# WHAT DID I DO LAST NIGHT?

# WHAT DID I DO LAST NIGHT?

## A DRUNKARD'S TALE

### BY TOM SYKES

Printed in the United States of America

Rodale Inc. makes every effort to use acid-free ⊗, recycled paper ◉.

Cover design by Tara Long

Interior design by Anthony Serge

Excerpt on pages 107–108 courtesy of the *New York Observer*

**Library of Congress Cataloging-in-Publication Data**

Sykes, Tom.
    What did I do last night? : a drunkard's tale / Tom Sykes.
       p.     cm.
    ISBN-13 978–1–59486–463–6 hardcover
    ISBN-10 1–59486–463–2 hardcover
    1. Sykes, Tom—Alcohol use.   2. Alcoholics—Rehabilitation—New York (State)
  3. Alcoholism—New York (State)  I. Title.
HV5068S95 2006
616.86'1092—dc22                                   2006019289
[B]

Distributed to the trade by Holtzbrinck Publishers

2  4  6  8  10  9  7  5  3  1  hardcover

LIVE YOUR WHOLE LIFE™

**We inspire and enable people to improve their lives and the world around them**

For more of our products visit **rodalestore.com** or call 800-848-4735

*For the Monk*

## ACKNOWLEDGMENTS

A giant thank-you to everyone who made this possible. First, my family: my wife, Sasha; my mother, Valerie; my sisters, Lucy, Plum, and Alice; my brothers, Fred and Josh; my father, Mark; and my brothers-in-law, Euan, Chris, and Toby. My work colleagues: Chris Wilson, for continuing to be the greatest man in the known world for a wild night out in New York City, and Paula Froelich, for introducing me to my editor, Leigh Haber, in the first place. Thanks to my friends, especially Rupert, "William," Robin, Neil, Olly, "Frank," Tom, "James," Helen, and Alex, for letting me use their stories and helping me remember all the nonsense we got up to. Thanks are also due to Luke Janklow, Rick Marin, Tracey Westmoreland, and Eddie B. And to James Frey for the importance of this statement: Everything in this book is absolutely true, although sequences have been rearranged and conversations re-created, often on the basis of subsequent interviews. The names of "James," "Brad," "Frank," "William Clarke," "Jim Jones," "Greg Davidson," and "Matthew Mole" are pseudonyms.

# PROLOGUE

## −3 DAYS

It was somewhere past midnight, and I was standing at the bar in Siberia, complaining that my martini seemed a bit weak.

"Patrick," I called out over the long wooden bar, "did you let the ice melt in this or something?"

"What?" sighed Patrick, the long-suffering barman. He pushed his long hair back from his face as he walked toward me. He was framed by a pyramid of glowing liquor bottles stacked behind him. "What's the matter, Tom?"

"It's this martini," I grumbled. "It doesn't seem to have any kick in it."

"No kick! It's pure vodka, man. That's what a martini is. A martini *can't be* weak."

"Maybe the ice melted."

"You want me to make you another?"

"No, no," I muttered. "It's fine. Whatever."

My best friend, Chris Wilson, with whom I worked on Page Six, the gossip column at the *New York Post* (where I also wrote a weekly column about the city's bar scene), was standing next to me at the bar.

"I find it's advisable to drink only prepackaged alcohol at Siberia," he opined sagely, taking a pull on his stubby bottle of Heineken.

He had a point. Siberia, a windowless cave located in the New

York district of Hell's Kitchen and on Fortieth Street between Eighth and Ninth avenues, was no cocktail lounge. It was, however, widely reckoned to be the best dive bar in New York, with a wealth of idiosyncratic details, like an old porcelain toilet slung by chains from the roof above the serving area, with a blow-up sex doll stuffed headfirst into the bowl, and two vintage Harley Davidsons parked in the middle of the bar. The wooden chipboard floor was coated with years of drink spillage. The liquid had evaporated to leave a mysterious viscous detritus the color and texture of molasses that was impossible to get off your clothes if you fell over. Siberia had no sign outside, just a small red bulb winking into the night. It all added up to a dubiously charming kind of appeal.

Anything went at Siberia, thanks in large part to its 266-pound, goatee-sporting owner, Tracey Westmoreland, who was just then striding through the swing door, bringing a blast of icy December air with him. I was always pleased to see Tracey, not least because he made sure his friends, especially those who wrote about nightlife for a living, drank for free.

He gave me a bear hug, too tight, verging on painful, as usual.

"Patrick," he called over the bar, pointing at me and Chris, "these guys are on a full scholarship."

"Cheers, mate," I said to Tracey as he disappeared to the other end of the bar. Then, to Patrick, my head spinning now, "Let me have another one of your martinis. Can you try and make it a little stronger this time?"

Patrick shrugged, his palms flat up in the air in despair.

The next two hours didn't come back to me until the following day. I walked around the bar, bitching about the insufficient potency of Patrick's martinis to anyone who would listen to me, my feet sticking to the gluey floor like a moonwalker's struggling with gravity. Then I was climbing over the counter, trying to get Patrick to switch off the jukebox and put an Ozzy Osbourne CD on the stereo behind the bar. I had been sent the CD at work and had been carrying it in my pocket all night.

He must have put it on, because the next thing I knew, I was dancing to Ozzy on the low stage that ran around the back wall of the bar. Colored lights were dazzling my eyes. I picked up an old metal chair and began playing air guitar to the song "Paranoid." The crowd roared. The world shifted half a degree, and suddenly I *was* Ozzy Osbourne, performing live to a sold-out crowd.

I gave my fans the rock salute and yelled, "Come on!" They screamed back their appreciation. But how could I, Ozzy Osbourne, take this performance to the next level?

The next thing I knew, everything went into slow motion, and I was twenty feet up in the air, looking down on the stage. And a guy in a Paul Smith shirt and APC jeans was swinging a chair high up in the air and bringing it down with astounding force over and over again on an old 1980s video arcade game, a Pac-Man machine that looked like a table; competitors sat on either side of it. Glass was flying; smoke was pouring out of the caved-in screen.

And I thought, *Who the hell is that guy?*

He lifted the chair above his head again. His hair was flying back with the momentum; his eyes were bloodshot red; and his wide-open mouth was letting out a frenzied, furious, bloodcurdling scream.

That was when I realized, with horror, that it was me. And if that was me, then what was I doing up here? Was I about to die?

I floated sickeningly above the stage, watching myself flail drunkenly among the glass and the metal and the smoke.

What had I become?

## −5,214 DAYS

My school had a pub, and I was pacing urgently across a cobbled courtyard toward it. It was the first day of the new term, the first day I was allowed to drink there, and I was late.

In England, the legal drinking age is eighteen; but at Eton College, you were allowed in the school bar, which was actually called Tap, at sixteen. The school circumvented the licensing laws by claiming Tap was a private social club. Technically, you were only allowed two pints of beer. In reality, you had to fall over before the locals who worked the pumps would cut you off. The beer at Tap was subsidized, so it was cheaper than at the pubs where we drank (with fake ID) during the holidays in London.

Tap was just one more unique oddity of being a student at Eton, soon to become the most famous boys' school in England when Princess Diana's sons, William and Harry, enrolled there. Some of the other, less enjoyable idiosyncracies included wearing a tailsuit to lessons every day (in mourning, more than five hundred years later, for the death of the school's founder, Henry VI, who was murdered in the Tower of London by Richard III in 1471); playing sports unknown outside the school walls (the field game, the wall game, and Eton fives); and having to learn a whole new language, where teachers were "beaks" and new boys were "tits." Fortunately, the ancient tradition of having to run errands for older boys, or "fagging," had recently been abolished. Tourists and parents considered these anachronisms quaint and charming. Three years in, I just thought they were normal.

Tap was open from 4:00 to 6:10 p.m. on Tuesdays and Thursdays and from 4:00 to 6:00 p.m. on Saturdays—when there was also "late Tap" from 8:00 to 10:15 p.m. for prefects. It was a privilege reserved for the senior boys in their final two years at Eton—"Upper School." For once, I couldn't wait to get back to Eton, although my delight was not only because I was excited to check out Tap.

I was also desperate to get away from home. Home was hell at the moment. Two years earlier—when I was fourteen—my mercurial father had abandoned my mother and his six children and run off to the south of France to become a born-again playboy. He never sent my mom any money to support his children, and as a result of all this, my mother had suffered a major nervous breakdown. Then the idyllic farmhouse in Kent, where I had grown up surrounded by nut orchards and rolling fields and which actually belonged to my grandmother, who lived there with us, had been sold to pay off my parents' debts. My mom was chronically broke and still in bed most of the time, my grandmother and various friends and relatives were paying my school fees, and home was now a rented cottage on my uncle's farm in Surrey. My older twin sisters, Plum and Lucy, had left home to go to university and drama school, respectively. Alice, who was two years older than I, had finished school and taken off to Europe on an extended vacation. My younger brother, Fred, was seven, a study in baffled melancholy; and my baby brother, Josh, who was three, had recently been hospitalized after eating handfuls of my mother's antidepressants in what I perceived to be a precocious suicide attempt.

I scratched my leg under the itchy pinstriped wool trousers as I sped toward Tap. I was relieved that Josh had recovered, but I kept wondering guiltily whether or not his death would have been enough to get my parents back together. As things stood, the Sykes family was well and truly fucked.

None of my friends at school really knew quite how desperate my home situation was. They knew about my dad leaving, of course, and that was embarrassing enough, but I hadn't made anyone familiar with the miserable updated details. Still, I was going to Tap for the first time, and the next couple of hours were going to be just fine.

I pushed through the swing doors of Tap into a scene of pandemonium. Hundreds of overprivileged sixteen-year-old boys were waving £50 notes and checkbooks at the bar staff and screaming for more and more alcohol. I pushed my way to the bar through a sea of black tailcoats.

"A pint of lager, please, Mrs. Cripps," I shouted at the barwoman. I already knew her name because in the mornings she worked in the tuck shop, which backed onto Tap, selling us bacon rolls.

I grabbed my pint off the bar and wriggled out of the crowd, looking around for my friends. They were sitting in a gang of about twenty on a leather banquette that skirted the corner of the room, and they were grinning like maniacs at their pints. I managed to sit down next to my friend William Clarke.

"Psycho! Where have you been?" he asked. William was well over six feet and built like an international rugby player, which was lucky for him.

"Harrison made me rake the bloody leaves off his lawn again," I said, swallowing beer as fast as I could and explaining why I had arrived at Tap half an hour after the opening bell. Dr. David Harrison was my housemaster, and I seemed to spend most of my free time clearing leaves off his lawn as punishment for one transgression or another. This time it was because I had started off the term badly by not unpacking all my cases properly and leaving my room in a mess.

The man was as fanatical about his garden as he was loathed by his students. These two defining facts about Dr. Death, as we called him, had come together recently when some boys in our house had crept out in the middle of the night and weed-killed a giant cock and balls on his prized half-moon lawn.

"Typical," said William. "That's so unfair. Today of all days." Then he looked around at the basic surroundings of Tap and said with all the excitement of a new initiate, "This is bloody amazing, isn't it? Is that your first pint?"

"Yep," I said. "But I've nearly finished it. I'm going to get another in a minute."

"I'm on my third," he said. "If I give you the money, can you get me one so I can line it up for when this one is finished?"

He had hardly made a dent in the drink he had, but I said, "Indeed." *Indeed* was my new favorite word. "Lager?"

"No. Newcastle Brown. In a jug." I stood up, trying not to let on I didn't know what he meant.

I fought my way back to the bar and ordered a Newcastle Brown for William and copied him, getting one for myself instead of a lager. "In jugs, please, Mrs. Cripps," I said hopefully. The beers were slammed on the bar in fat, handled, windowed glasses that were easy to carry through the melee.

"This is great, isn't it?" I said for about the fiftieth time as I sat down next to William again. "Can you believe how cheap it is? I can't believe we get cheap beer."

After two more pints, my head was spinning. The place looked like a cross between a tuck shop and a gin mill. The bathrooms stank of vomit. Boys in tailsuits were sitting in stupefied dazes all around the edge of the room, long hair flopping over their pale, pimpled faces. I saw my friend Gerry, who was in the year above me.

"How many pints have you had?" I shouted.

"Seven," he burped beerily. "Usually I forget how many I've had, but today I've been drawing them on my hand so that I won't." He proudly stuck out his hand, covered in inky caricatures of the squat beer glasses William had asked to be served in. Deeply impressed, I clapped him on the back. One day, I swore, I would be able to drink that much.

At 6:10 p.m., Tap closed. This was so the boys could get back to their boardinghouses in time for quiet hour, the study period that started at 6:15 every night and lasted till dinner at 7:30. Today, there wasn't going to be much work going on.

I trooped back to my boardinghouse with William and my eight other housemates. One good thing about Eton was that everyone got their own room, complete with a desk and a hinged bed that you had to strap the mattress to and fold up into the wall every morning before breakfast. You could decorate your room however you liked. My walls were covered in Pink Floyd posters and ethnic-print drapes.

I had drunk four pints, and my head was spinning, but I resisted the temptation to pull my bed down from the wall and lie on it, in case Dr. Harrison came barging in to check up on me. I didn't want to do any more leaf sweeping. I sat at the wooden desk in the corner by the window with my hands over my eyes.

Eton was a confusing place. Just six months previously I had been "rusticated" (suspended from school, as in, "sent home to the country") for five days after William and I had been caught buying vodka in Windsor, the nearest big town. Yet now I was allowed to drink. And although the school pub seemed happy enough to serve me until I fell over, I knew I would be in big trouble if I actually did fall over and Harrison discovered how drunk I was.

Getting money for drinking sessions was no problem. Although my dad never supported my mother, he was in the habit of sending me occasional but extravagant checks from his hidey-hole in the south of France. They were often accompanied by bizarre jokes or cartoons. One that I remember said, "I went to the theater the other night and the following rhyme occurred to me. 'If Federico Garcia Lorca/Had been born a pig/He would have been called Federico Garcia Porca." In another letter, a cartoon showed a smug gentleman orbiting the earth, leaning back in an armchair with a glass of port and a cigar, his slippered feet stretched out on a stool. The earth was exploding. My dad had written the caption "The End of the World Viewed in Comfort" underneath.

The one thing I could guarantee was that my dad's letters would never address the one thing that mattered. Whenever I wrote letters that demanded to know why he had left my mom, I would usually receive a short note in return, saying something like "It became impossible for your mother and I to continue living together," with a check for £500, sometimes even £1,000.

Although I tried not to, I missed my dad. Dad was an incredible storyteller and raconteur. When I was little, one of my favorite games was getting him to list his jobs. He had been an avocado farmer in East Timor and a racing driver in Australia. In the Vietnam War, he had sold blankets to the Viet Cong. He had started a nightclub in London (the Wag in Soho—it's still there), run lucrative illegal gambling operations in England and Australia, reported on the French Foreign Legion spearing babies to doorposts with bayonets in Algeria, and even smuggled weapons to support the Arabs in their insurrection against the French in North Africa. Often, he would hint darkly that he had killed a man. When we drove down the country lanes from our house to the nearest town, Sevenoaks, he would sneak up behind pheasants in the car, sound his horn, then whack into them with the windscreen, with us children screaming with excitement in the backseat. We'd pick up the dead birds on the way home, once they had stopped twitching, and my mom's old nanny, Winnie, who still worked for my granny, would pluck them and cook them for dinner. Being with Dad was thrilling.

The last time I really saw my father was on Remembrance Day,

November 11, the day the country pauses for two minutes of silence at 11:00 a.m. to honor the war dead. It was 1988, and I was fourteen. Dad drove to Eton with my sister Plum for the service on the morning of Remembrance Day—he was driving her to Oxford, where she was at university.

The service sticks in my memory because it was a weekday, twenty minutes in the chapel before school—basically an assembly with prayers. Parents never came to these services. They came to the hour-long services on a Sunday instead. I kept wondering for days afterward why Dad had come to chapel at Eton in midweek.

I have seen my father many times since then, but that was the last time I saw him before everything changed. Even on that day I had a sense that things were changing. My dad looked older, fatter, different somehow. I noticed that his hair was dyed a lighter brown than usual. Plum looked older too—but in a more positive way. Plum had been shy, serious, and nervous as a teenager. Since leaving school and going to Oxford that year, she had become newly confident, and her whole presence was transformed. She was beautiful, thin, with strong features and long hair.

Because Plum was with my dad, they were seated at the front of the chapel on a dais reserved for dignitaries. I could just see the Lower Master thinking, *Yes, yes, that's a fine idea! Let's seat this girl somewhere prominent, somewhere all our female-deprived boys can see a beautiful young woman! That'll be some first-class entertainment for them!*

I can't remember anything of the service beyond their presence or much of the weeks that followed. But soon after, there was a four-day holiday, "Short Leave." When I got home to the farmhouse in Kent, the horrible truth emerged.

My father had sent nearly all the valuable furniture, paintings, and antiques in our house to be "restored." All his suits had gone to the "dry cleaner." I can imagine him scooping up every last two-piece out of his cupboard, saying, "Time to get everything cleaned!" and loading up all the suits into the car and driving them away. Then he packed his few remaining belongings and announced he was off to the south of France on a business trip.

The suits never returned from the dry cleaner. And although a few pieces of furniture were sent back, the paintings were gone for good too. Sometimes, when I visit him these days, I'll see one of the pictures that disappeared from my childhood hanging on his wall, and I'll remember how their removal left nothing but very neat squares of very clean paint underneath.

"You're the man of the house now," my grandmother told me, and I nodded dumbly in agreement, baffled at how quickly my world had fallen apart.

That Christmas, my father came back for a few days, but the knowledge of his ongoing affairs in London became too much for my mother to bear. In the end, it was she who told him to leave.

When I got back to school in the new year of 1989, I was ashamed to admit to my friends that my family had broken up. I was fourteen, and I didn't want to be an object of pity. I felt like a fraud in the perfect world of Eton, where everyone else's parents were rich, happy, and together. At Eton, broken homes were something that happened to other people.

To make matters even worse, one of the women my father had chosen to have an affair with was a close relative of "the Dame," the middle-aged, gray-haired spinster who acted as house matron and lived in a small upstairs apartment in my boardinghouse.

She came into my room one night before lights-out and sat on the edge of my bed in her starched blue uniform, stroking the bedcovers, unable to look me in the eye.

Eventually she said, in her prim Scottish accent, "I know things are difficult at the moment, Tom, and I feel terrible because it involves my family."

I just lay there, half-sitting up in bed, desperately wishing she would go away because I had hurriedly thrust a copy of *Penthouse* down the side of my bed when she walked in.

"It's not your fault," I said.

"Just remember that there are two people in the world who love you," she said.

"I'm not so sure about that," I said, trying not to cry.

She sat on my bed for another long minute, picking the fluff off my blanket. Eventually she stood up. She seemed to be searching for some words that might make it all better. There were none.

"Well, I am sorry," she said. "If you ever want to talk, you know you can come up to my flat anytime."

"Yes, ma'am," I said. She got up to leave, gave me a thin smile, and shut the door behind her. I sank into my pillow, groaning with humiliation and shame, the porn quite forgotten.

A few days later, on the first weekend of the spring term, I got drunk for the first time on a couple of cans of Special Brew, a viscous lager favored by tramps for its formidable alcohol content. William had smuggled them into school. A group of four of us drank two cans each in another boy's room. All our rooms were painted a vivid shade of yellow, and this one was no exception, so we covered a bedside lamp with a piece of cloth to "mellow out."

The taste of the beer made me retch a few times, but I got used to it before I was halfway through the can. William "shotgunned" his second can, punching a hole in the side with a knife and clamping his lips around the wound. With his head sideways and the beer can held upright, someone else opened the ring pull. William drank the contents in a matter of seconds. We all cheered as he let out a giant burp.

I gave shotgunning a go with my second can. I had to swallow beer furiously from the moment the ring pull was opened, but the good thing was that I could only taste bubbles because the beer was flowing so fast. Afterward I felt sick.

It was great.

No one was laughing at me because of my dad anymore. I had a gang now, a bunch of friends. These four guys with whom I was lying on the floor, giggling, spinning gently, trusted me enough, liked me enough, to include me. I knew I was drunk, and I loved it. In fact, I was already planning how to get more beer the following weekend.

## −5,100 DAYS

Tap was a clear improvement on the tuck shop, but it had its limitations. For starters, it was open for only a few hours a day, which was enough time to get drunk if you moved fast but was not conducive to a really good session. Second, you couldn't smoke at Tap, and I liked to smoke when I drank. And third, I missed the thrill of breaking the rules. So I carried on going over the bridge to Windsor to go to the pubs or buy booze to drink on the playing fields with whomever I could persuade to accompany me.

You had to be careful not to let on you were an Etonian in the Windsor pubs. The younger residents would eye us suspiciously. Their cheap clothes marked them as poor, violent, and, we assumed, itching to hang an Etonian scalp on their wall.

After being rusticated for buying vodka with William, I tried to purchase my alcohol at unusual locations. One of my favorite spots to buy booze was a French wine outlet store called Bordeaux Direct, located in a refurbished railway arch in Windsor. I cut through the pockets of my overcoat so I could carry two bottles of wine back to school in its lining. I felt so smart as I grinned good day to the beaks I passed on the street on my way back to my house.

William's enthusiasm for hanging out with me was starting to wane a little, especially after we were caught buying the vodka, and my new best friend was another boy in my house called Rupert Neville. Rupert lived near me at home, so we saw each other during the holidays. As well as drinking, he also liked smoking cigarettes and gambling on the horses—neither of which was William's thing.

Over drinks in a Windsor pub one Saturday afternoon when we were supposed to be playing rugby, Rupert became conspiratorial.

"Harrison made me move some of his shitty old furniture into the cellar the other day," he said, pushing his big glasses up his nose.

"Oh, yeah?" I said, unsurprised. Being corralled into doing your housemaster's menial labor was nothing new.

"Yeah. And I noticed that he keeps his wine down there."

I looked at Rupert intently. "Really? Could we get it?"

"Well, I don't know," Rupert said, thoughtfully stirring his drink—a brandy and ginger ale—and lighting yet another self-rolled cigarette. We both smoked roll-ups. "There's a locked gate in front of it, but it's like a big grid, and some of the wine is near the front."

"And?"

"I think we could reach it."

That was all I needed to hear. The next night, before we went to bed, we set our alarm clocks for 3:00 a.m. When the alarm went off, I silenced it immediately and got out of bed, dressing in a pair of jeans, sneakers, and my long overcoat to keep out the cold. I crept down the passageway and met Rupert in the big bathroom on our floor, as we had arranged. He was wearing his dark red dressing gown and holding a flashlight. We gave each other a thumbs-up sign, then crept down the main stairs of the house in total silence.

The entrance to the cellar was via a small, tightly sprung door, which gave directly onto another set of very steep, narrow stairs. As we tiptoed down them, I tried not to think how much trouble I would be in if I were caught. I would almost certainly be expelled. I should have been being extra careful, because just a few months before, I had been arrested for riding my sister's motorbike on the roads during the school holidays. I was fifteen—too young to have a license—and drunk, and the school had found out when I had to go to court in term time. They didn't take it well. I would definitely lose the bursary that paid half my fees if I were busted now, which amounted to the same thing as being thrown out anyway, I reflected, standing on the top step and wondering if it was too late to turn back.

"Psycho! Come on!" whispered Rupert. He was standing on the stairs in the darkness, turning back to me.

I liked the romance of being a rebel. My dad had been a rebel when he was at Eton. One of the most important buildings in Eton was the imposing school library with an old cannon in the railed courtyard opposite it. My dad had told me that when he was at Eton, he and a friend had filled the cannon with bread rolls and blasted the library with them in the dead of night, using homemade dynamite that they had manufactured in the science schools. Another of his classic stories was about driving around the town with his rich friend who kept a Rolls-Royce at a garage in Eton. My dad would do an impression of how they drove up and down the high street, his arms extended above his head, grasping the imaginary steering wheel. They hid beneath the dashboard whenever they saw an authority figure and used a mirror to view the road like submarine commanders.

Rupert shone the light in my face. "Come on!" he whispered again.

I went.

The cellar was very dusty and full of cobwebs. By the sweep of Rupert's flashlight, I could see piles of old furniture and broken benches and chairs, familiar in design from the house assembly room. And there, in one corner, under a vaulted arch and behind a locked metal grid, was the holy grail—Dr. Harrison's wine cellar.

The metal grid protecting the wine looked like it had been made several hundred years ago. It was medieval: big, wide strips of metal bolted together with screws. It was easy enough to reach your arm through, and, as Rupert had predicted, we were comfortably able to reach the outermost bottles. My heart was racing as I stretched my arm through the grid and slowly extracted one bottle after another. I took four in all, two for each of us.

Then we started back up the stairs. We held a bottle by the neck in each fist to stop them clinking. If we were caught now, we were dead. But the house was sleeping, dark and silent. We eased back the spring door, shut it behind us as quietly as we could, and tiptoed up the stairs. We hid the bottles in our rooms until the weekend, then snuck off to an island in the middle of the river that ran through the school to drink them.

It was the best wine I have ever tasted, before or since. Not that we cared about the quality. The point was that we'd stuck it to the man.

Over the next few months, I developed an unquenchable thirst for Dr. Harrison's wine. Once I even sold some of the bottles I had stolen to some other boys and just went back for more the next night. For the many months this went on, it was as if we had discovered a goose that laid golden eggs. But it had to come to an end. One night, we got down there and discovered that someone—either he or a member of his staff—must have realized what was going on and moved all the bottles to the back of the cellar, out of reach of our arms.

We were incensed, outraged, but we quickly came up with a plan. The next night, I met Rupert in the bathroom. In addition to a flashlight, he was also carrying a pop-out umbrella, a bamboo stick, and a piece of string with a small loop at the end of it, like a lasso. We snuck down to the cellar for the last time and by flashlight began our most daring heist yet.

In silence, I used the bamboo stick to guide the flimsy lasso over the necks of the bottles beyond our reach. Then I pulled the string tight with a few sharp jerks while Rupert pushed the folded umbrella through the grate. He pressed a button on the handle to extend it. It shot open with a tremendous amount of noise. Then he held the umbrella under the lassoed bottle, and I gently pulled the wine out of the rack. It plopped into the umbrella. The umbrella held the weight of the bottle, and we sighed with relief. We took six bottles of wine that night. We couldn't extricate the umbrella because we couldn't fold it up again to get it out of the grid, so we just left it there. As we snuck up the stairs with our haul for the last time, I was thrilled by our ingenuity. I shone the flashlight back at the abandoned umbrella and suddenly understood why burglars like to take a crap in their victims' living rooms. There's really no better way to say "fuck you."

I began to buy cannabis regularly. I would buy lumps of hashish (at vastly inflated prices, I later found out) from a Rastafarian who lived on the Portobello Road near Notting Hill. I financed my habit easily using my father's occasional but extravagant checks.

Back at school, Rupert and I would sneak out of the house most nights to smoke dope in the subterranean World War II bomb shelter we had discovered at the bottom of my housemaster's garden. The happiest days of my school career were spent skinning up giant joints in the bomb shelter—which we dubbed the Nostril because of its cylindrical shape. The Nostril was decorated with tatty drapes nailed or stuck onto the concrete walls; and we sat in old chairs, sometimes as many as ten of us, a band of renegades on the lam from the bizarre world above. Down there I could drift away in a haze of dope smoke, freed from all my worries by marijuana. I adored the Nostril. I spent hours there every night, listening to reggae on the crappy stereo and patching up wax leaks on the menhir-sized candles.

Above ground I was a failure, ashamed of my parents' brutal estrangement, ashamed that my father apparently didn't care about me, ashamed by my family's relative poverty; and, to add insult to injury, I was useless at sport. But down there, I was normal. Most of my friends who spent time with me in the Nostril hated and were hated by the school as much as I was. I belonged to a group, a gang. What's more, I had developed a genuine talent for skinning up really big reefers. This rebel stuff was something I could be good at.

On my very last weekend at Eton, I went out drinking with William again. I furtively opened a bottle of wine from Bordeaux Direct under the railway arches with two girls we had met from a nearby boarding school. We drank one bottle, then invited them back to our house to drink some more.

I don't know what we were thinking, why we didn't just drink the wine on the playing fields somewhere. But for some reason, we took the girls back to my room. We hadn't even gotten to the stage of getting their clothes off when we heard the sound of Dr. Harrison charging around the house, flinging open doors, shouting, "SYKES! CLARKE!"

All four of us looked at one another in a panic.

"Quick! We've got to get you out of here," I shouted.

We ran down the corridor and bustled the girls out of the back entrance to the house. Then we heard Dr. Harrison yelling our names again. William and I split up and ran to the top of the house up different staircases. Dr. Harrison followed me.

"SYKES! STOP!"

Just like that, I stopped, no longer a rebel, just another frightened and slightly drunk overprivileged little boy. Dr. Harrison caught up with me; his face was bright red, and he was shaking with rage. I looked out the window and saw the girls hurrying down the driveway.

He followed my gaze, then turned to me with a nasty expression on his face, his eyes burning over the tops of his half-moon glasses, and said, "If those girls have been in the house, Sykes, you're for the long walk!"

He sprinted down the stairs at an impressive pace for a man in late middle age. From the window, I watched him grab the girls and march them back to our house.

## −5,020 DAYS

*March 20, 1991*

*Dear Valerie,*

*For the record, I send you Thomas's reports for the half, written mostly before disaster struck. Somewhere he has a copy of* Manon Lescaut *from the school library, which the school librarian would be glad to have back.*

*I also send you his GCSE etc certificates, which he will need if he wants further education (or some jobs). They must be kept in a safe place!*

*I gather from Jeremy Nichols that you thought Stowe might suit Thomas. I feel bound to say that there might be an element of danger in this; Thomas might find the constraints there as frustrating as Eton's and the intellectual stimulation, to offset them, a good deal less.*

*With Best Wishes,*

*Yours Sincerely,*

*David*

## −5,025 DAYS

I packed up my room at Eton like I was being evicted. I tore down a huge blue drape from the wall and simply threw all my possessions into it. Books, clothes, letters—everything went into the drape. My friends stood around the doorway to my room, looking as horrified as they were thrilled by the unfolding drama.

"What happened?" Rupert said.

What had happened was that the headman, Eric Anderson, had rung our home—the rented cottage on my uncle's estate—the night before and asked my mom to come up to the school with me the next day. At that point, I had only been rusticated, albeit for a staggering three weeks, for the wine-and-girls-in-the-house episode. So we had driven up to Eton the following day. I was fairly sure I was about to be expelled—I knew this was the way it usually happened—but Mom seemed blissfully unaware of my impending doom.

"I'm just going to tell Mr. Anderton that he's *got* to let you stay," was all she would say when I suggested the meeting was likely to end with me getting the boot. We were whizzing round the motorway at about 90 miles per hour, and my mom was driving barefoot, as usual.

"It's Anderson, Mom, not Anderton. Eric Anderson."

"All right, Anderson. I mean, they've *got* to keep you. They *know* what we have been through as a family. They can't just wash their hands of you! Now eat some of this flapjack. It's got sunflower seeds in it. It'll be great for your immune system."

I gazed listlessly out of the window at the familiar scenery flashing by, the resilience of my immune system not preeminent in my mind.

"And, I mean, they can't just get rid of you after you were the star of that television program," Mom said. I shuddered. A documentary had just been made about Eton life, and one scene—which pointed up how modern Eton's syllabus was—featured me murdering a few words of basic Japanese.

"*Konichiwa!*" I said, bowing to the camera.

In a supreme irony, it had been shown just days ago. My poor mother had to endure dozens of phone calls from her friends congratulating her on *how well* I was doing despite the turmoil at home, while I sat as quietly as possible in another corner of the room.

"I mean . . ."

"Look out!" I screamed as we nearly rammed into the back of an eighteen-wheeler.

My mom didn't blink. She dabbed the brakes, and then hit the accelerator again, overtaking on the inside, turning her head ninety degrees to smile at me. I shut my eyes and gripped the handrest.

Mom's cars were always covered in dents. Usually I thought this was funny. I even took a perverse pride in them, evidence as they were of her indifference to bourgeois social conventions such as panel beating.

But when we pulled up outside the headman's office, a luxurious suite of rooms, each the size of a soccer pitch, housed in one of the school's oldest buildings, my mom's dented Nissan seemed just another embarrassing indictment, a reminder that people like us really had no business being at Eton in the first place.

I sat in one room adjacent to the headman's office while my mom went into the other to see him. I sat there for half an hour. His secretary never looked up from her computer. I couldn't hear a word from inside the office. No sound from inside the office escaped the thick wool carpet or the solid oak doors.

Eventually she came out, shaking her head and just saying, "No, no, it's no good, no good," over and over again. She looked washed out.

I hugged her and said, "Mom, I'm so sorry."

Then we went to my house, neither of us in tears but both of us on the verge of them, where I went up to my room; shoved everything in that drape; told Rupert, "I got kicked out"; grabbed the four corners of my giant bundle; and half-pushed, half-carried the whole lot angrily down the stairs and forced it into the trunk of the car.

On the staircase wall, I noticed on the way down that somebody had already scratched "TOM SYKES RIP." I climbed into the passenger seat and gritted my teeth.

We sped back round the motorway for the last time in a bubble of loaded silence. Eventually I coughed and asked, "So what did he say?"

"He was *horrible*," my mom said, dabbing at her eyes now, the walls beginning to come down. "He just kept telling me over and over again that you needed to see a psychiatrist."

I didn't mention to Mom that I had actually been to see the school shrink at Eton. It hadn't gone well. I had burst into tears and sobbed, "My dad . . . my dad . . ." At the end of an hour of this, the psychiatrist had said, "You're a very unhappy boy, Tom. And I am afraid that I can't just wave a magic wand and make all this disappear." I made another appointment, but I never went back. What would have been the point?

My mom was still talking about the headman's treatment of her. "He was so cold. He just wanted me *out* of that office. He kept telling me, 'You must leave this office now, Mrs. Sykes.' And I said, 'No! Just talk to me, Mr. Anderton.' I wouldn't leave."

Oh, my God, she had actually called him Anderton instead of Anderson. Good.

"He wouldn't even talk to me. He just wanted me *out*."

"Thanks, Mom," I said. "I'm so sorry."

We lapsed into silence for another half hour.

"So what do you want to do?" my mother asked eventually, her voice quivering.

I had absolutely no idea what I wanted to do, but I thought I'd better say something. I was racked with guilt about what this latest disaster would do to her health. I wanted to be strong for her.

"I'll get a job," I said. "That way I can pay my way, be of use."

"How will you get a job?" asked my mother. It was a reasonable question. At sixteen, I had a bunch of basic qualifications, but still, I was hardly a killer hire.

I thought for a few seconds. "I'll go to the job center. You can drop me off there on the way home."

An hour later, she pulled into the car park at the job center in Redhill, the big town near our house.

"I'll get a train home," I said as I got out of the car.

She drove off crying.

*Christ.* I felt awful. Despite her depression and illness, my mom had summoned all her last reserves of energy to make the trip to Eton to try to keep me in the school. Now that she had failed, it was as if she had sunk lower than ever. And it was all my fault. Or my dad's fault, depending on how you looked at it.

When the car was out of sight, I walked over to a newsagent and bought a packet of cigarettes. I cupped a match smoothly in my hand to light one and smoked it thoughtfully, pacing around the pedestrianized town center. I walked past a pub. I decided to duck in for a pint. Well, I could now, couldn't I? This was the whole point.

I flashed my fake ID and sat at the bar in the smoky pub, thinking about my options. I had two: Either I could get a job or I could go back to school. Going back to school would be difficult—there was no money to pay for me to go to a private school. The fees at Eton had only been manageable because of my bursary. The thought of going to a state school filled me with terror. At Eton I had been trained to fear the masses. I was pretty certain that I wouldn't survive more than a day or two outside the private system without being hospitalized.

But if I got a job, well, I would have money. I could go to pubs as much as I wanted. And I could smoke cigarettes and weed whenever the mood took me as well. Freedom—it sounded good. I thought of my dad and his never-ending résumé. Maybe I could work on an avocado farm in Tibet? Become a weapons dealer? I wondered if my dad knew I had been expelled, then realized, *Of course not, of course he doesn't.* No one had been in touch after all.

A guy in his twenties was sitting at the bar next to me. I ordered another pint and leaned across to him.

"Excuse me?" I asked in my cut-glass English accent.

"Yeah?" said the guy. He was wearing a chef's jacket, and he had two yellowing front teeth and two days' worth of stubble on his face.

"Can I ask you a question? Do you have any academic qualifications?"

"No," said the bloke. He reacted to my question as if I had just asked him if he was an ax murderer. "What's it to you?"

"Well, I've just been expelled from school, and I was wondering whether I should get a job or go back to school."

The guy sighed, offered me one of his cigarettes, took a long draw on his, and exhaled a blast of smoke in my direction. I took one and lit it.

"Right," he said. "I passed you in the street just a few minutes earlier, and you nearly knocked me off my feet. Looked like you didn't know where you were going."

"Sorry about that."

"Yeah, well, I could tell you looked a bit out of it. A bit spaced out."

I told him the whole story.

He nodded while I talked. When I got to the end, I offered to buy him a pint.

"Yeah. Right. Lovely. Stella, please."

We were getting on like a house on fire now. Maybe it was not the case that anyone without a posh accent would want to kick my head in after all.

"Okay," I said, ordering the drinks, "so what would you do?"

"Well," he said slowly, pondering his pronouncement prophetically. "I'd say fuck it and have a laugh. Doesn't sound to me like you want to go back to that Eton place anyway. I mean, it's good about the pub there and all, but it sounds like it's full of fucking faggots to me. Go and get a job! I started working when I was sixteen, and, you know, at least that way you've always got a few quid in your pocket. You know, get some girls and that."

I thanked him, finished my pint, and walked over to the job center. I took a ticket and waited in line to see an employment advisor.

The employment advisor turned out to be a bored thirty-year-old woman who kept filing her nails throughout our brief interview. Every opportunity she got, she would make a tutting noise and roll her eyes to indicate that I was wasting her time and she was way above all this anyway.

"I need a job," I told her. Tut. Eye roll.

"I have ten GCSEs." Tut. Eye roll. Silence.

Eventually, she spoke. "Ever worked before?" she asked.

"No," I said. She sighed heavily, rummaged around her desk for a few moments, and then pulled out a job card.

"Strawberries," she said, pushing the card over to me.

I looked at the card. It was an opportunity to join a fast-growing fruit wholesaling firm, working as a key provider of raw product to the distribution chain.

It took a moment for the penny to drop. "You want me to pick strawberries?" I asked. "But wait a minute. I've got ten GCSEs in English, Math, Science, Latin. . . . Is there nothing else available? Something in an office?"

"Can you type?" she asked with a sigh.

"No," I said.

"Then it's strawberries," she said. "Take it or leave it." She exhaled dramatically and looked at her watch.

It paid £7 per hour. I took it.

## −5,024 DAYS

Strawberries are the summer totem of the moneyed classes in England. The newspapers report with glee how many tons of them will be devoured at sporting events like the Wimbledon tennis championships and the Henley rowing regatta. They are overpriced and served in little foam bowls with a dollop of cream and a sprinkling of sugar. They are piled up into huge pyramids at weddings as signifiers of good fortune, harbingers of financial security.

But at seven in the morning after my interview at the job center, as I stood in the middle of a vast strawberry field, plants stretching as far as the eye could see, wondering what had happened to my life, I hated strawberries. They mocked me.

Ten days earlier, I had been wearing a tailsuit and studying Shakespeare. Now, clad in a pair of old jeans and a dispensable white T-shirt, I couldn't help feeling a little sorry for myself as I bent over and began working my way down the line of plants, one foot planted on either side of the row.

I had been picking for about thirty minutes when the supervisor came past me and inspected my basket. He was a middle-aged man with a bushy black moustache, and even in the open air he stank of fermenting fruit.

"What the fuck do you call this then?" he said, nudging my basket with the tip of his Wellington boot.

"Er, well," I started, but he cut me off.

"A bloody waste of money, that's what it is!" he bellowed at me.

All around the giant field, with the pale early morning sun rising in the east, the other workers were standing up, hands on their hips, taking a break to watch the entertainment.

"Look at these. They are all mush!" he said, picking up one of the strawberries in my basket. It was falling apart because I hadn't picked it properly. I had left the stalk behind on the plant. "I can't sell that. That's no good for nothing but...jam. You'd better pick your game up, sonny, or you'll be out on your ass."

"Sorry," I muttered as he wandered on down the line. "I'm new."

He turned back and yelled, "I don't care if you're the king of England. If you can't pick a sodding strawberry, you're no good to me."

About eleven o'clock, we had a break. I drank a can of Coke as all the workers congregated on a patch of grass between the strawberry fields and the raspberry plants we were about to move on to. I sucked my fingers, stained red with strawberry juice.

A tough-looking guy with a shaved head and tattoos on his knuckles walked up to me. "So what you doing here?" he asked. I was transfixed as he professionally rolled up and lit a cigarette in a fraction of a second.

"I just got expelled from school," I said, trying to roughen up my accent a little. "What about you?"

"Just got out," he said.

"Oh. Out of where?" I asked innocently. He looked to be in his midthirties.

He paused for a long moment, drew his chin down to his neck, and frowned at me. "Prison," he said disdainfully.

"Oh, right," I said as casually as I could, as if I hung out with ex-cons every day of the week. "What were you in for?"

He looked at me for an even longer moment. "Manslaughter," he said. Then he stuck out his hand. "I'm Tony."

## −5,010 DAYS

Tony turned out to be a pretty cool guy. At the end of my second week, when I got my first pay packet, Tony gave me a lift to the pub. He threw my bicycle that I used to get to and from the farm in the back of his beat-up old pickup truck and drove violently at knuckle-whitening speed to a rough pub a few miles away. Because we started work so early, we were finished by two thirty, drinking our first pints in the beer garden—a grand name for what was actually a patch of roughly paved space out back. Traffic on a main road, hidden by a stained black fence, roared by noisily a few yards behind us. The garden smelled of the steam from the dishwasher we could hear clanking away in the kitchen, which jutted out of the main building.

We bitched about the strawberry farm and the supervisor for a little bit, then the conversation inexorably turned to our past lives.

"So you just got expelled from school, right?" he asked. Flush with his pay packet, Tony was smoking normal cigarettes instead of roll-ups today. "Straights," he called them.

"Yeah," I said, and I told him some stories about Eton. When I finished, he laughed and said, "Well, first time I ever had a pint with an old Etonian."

"First time I ever had a pint with a manslaughterer," I chanced, emboldened by the beer, and we both laughed, tipping our heads back to feel the sun.

Tony didn't get into the details about his crime, but he was happy to tell me about the prisons where he had been "banged up." We sat in the garden and drank pint after pint that sunny afternoon, as Tony told me how he made alcohol in his cell by fermenting oranges underneath his bed.

"I was fucking good at making orange wine," he kept repeating. "I was famous for it. I never went short. Cigarettes, porn, dope . . . I could always trade my wine for whatever I wanted. I was famous for it. I was fucking good at making orange wine."

Somewhere around the sixth pint, I became aware that Tony was stuck in an alcoholic loop, repeating himself over and over again. It freaked me out a little bit because I had drunk the same amount as he had. I went into the pub to take a piss.

It was pitch-black inside after the bright light outside. I stumbled down some steps, and the barwoman looked up sharply from her newspaper behind the bar.

"You all right?" she asked, her tone accusatory, not concerned. I was transfixed by her cigarette smoke coiling up from the ashtray on the bar, ethereal in the beams of sunlight that came in through the leaded windows.

"Yes," I said and stumbled blindly toward the bathroom.

In the bathroom, I had a piss, then leaned against the wall over the sink, my hands on either side of the mirror. I touched my forehead to the glass and grinned at my reflection. I thought of all my old friends at Eton. I checked my watch. They would just be finishing lessons about now. I pitied them their long weekend, trying to dodge the school authorities to get drunk.

This was life. What would I rather be doing—homework or swapping stories with a bona fide killer over a packet of cigarettes and six pints of Stella? I looked at myself in the mirror and said, "You're free. You're free."

I spent the weekend quietly at home. The following Monday, as I picked up my collecting basket at the strawberry farm, I looked around for Tony. He was nowhere to be seen. All the rest of the week, he didn't show up. I finally saw him on Friday, when he turned up to get his pay for the previous week.

"Sod this for a laugh," he said as he collected his money in a brown paper envelope. "I've got better things to do with my life than pick strawberries. Wanna go to the pub?"

Sure. I always wanted to go to the pub.

## −4,996 DAYS

Two weeks later, I was fired from the strawberry farm for taking a pot of cream to work with me, sitting down on my break, and eating the produce.

"What do you think this is?" the fermented fruit–smelling supervisor yelled when he saw me reclining on the mud between the furrows, a juicy, cream-coated strawberry on its way to my lips. "Fucking Wimbledon?"

That afternoon I sat in the bathtub at home for over an hour, trying to get the red off my fingers and considering my options afresh.

My back ached from crouching over all day, every day. I was exhausted. I had saved a grand total of £150. I was only sixteen, but still, I realized 150 quid wasn't going to get me very far. Maybe the chef I had spoken to was wrong. Maybe this work stuff wasn't all it was cracked up to be.

I was thinking the unthinkable: *Maybe I should go back to school.*

## −4,976 DAYS

One of the smartest things I ever did after I got fired from the strawberry farm was make an appointment to see the headmaster at my
local public school—or state school, as it is known in England—and
beg to be allowed to enroll there, even though by then it was spring
break, over halfway through the academic year, and just a few days
before the summer term was due to begin.

Initially the headmaster, Roger Coles, a bearded man in his fifties, insisted that I would have to repeat a year because the syllabi at
Eton and Oxted were not the same.

I told him that if I had to wait, I probably wouldn't go back to
school. He looked at the history teacher, Mr. Pickford, who was sitting in on our interview in Mr. Coles's small, file-cluttered office,
which was roughly one-tenth the size of Eric Anderson's. Mr. Pickford, the head of history, which was one of my subjects, had a giant
nose and wild, curly hair that was so long it was on the point of
becoming an Afro.

"Well, he's probably done more than most of our kids," said Mr.
Pickford with a heavy nasal twang. "So I say, come on down."

"All right then," said Mr. Coles. He pushed a scrap of photocopied
paper with the dates of the new term written on it toward me.

"Monday, 15 April," I read out loud, elated. "Thank you so much.
I'll see you then."

"Oh, no, no," said Mr. Coles. "Actually, that's wrong. Term actually starts on Tuesday."

"Oh, okay," I said, a little confused. I looked from him to Mr. Pickford. "See you on Tuesday then."

It wasn't till later that I found out that term had indeed started on Monday, as it said on the photocopy. But Mr. Coles hadn't wanted me there on Monday, because on Monday, the first day of term, he had gone into morning assembly and given the school a pep talk, using me as its basis.

He stood in front of the whole school and said, "This is the best state school in the whole of Surrey! And do you know how I know that? Because tomorrow we've got an old Etonian joining us!" He didn't, of course, mention that I had been expelled from Eton in disgrace.

Meanwhile, I was at home, working out what I was going to wear and perfecting my new, tougher accent that I had been working on the last few weeks.

I was terrified that I was going to be beaten to a pulp. One of my only friends who didn't go to Eton was Tom Freud. Our parents had been friends. Tom lived in London and went to a seriously rough state school.

I phoned him to ask his advice. How should I handle myself?

"Well," he said thoughtfully, "I think the mistake new kids make is that they try and be part of the gang right away. Like we have this game, when we are eating our lunch, to all try and push each other off this step. And this new guy turned up last term and right away he was trying to push us off the step. He was too quick to try and jump in. You know, you've got to play it cool. You'll be fine, Tommy."

*Don't push anyone off a step*, I thought to myself as I cycled to school the next day. *Play it cool, and you'll be fine.*

About 2,500 students, the same number as Eton, attended Oxted County School, but that was where the similarities ended. Instead of being spread out over a town, with schoolrooms housed in centuries-old buildings, Oxted County conducted its pedagogy in several modern structures squeezed into a couple of cramped acres on the edge of the town. When the bell rang at the end of lessons, there were human traffic jams in the playgrounds as the kids tried to get to their next class. Famous old boys at Eton included Percy Bysse Shelley and Pitt the Younger. At Oxted, our most notable alumnus was believed to be one of the great train robbers. It wasn't even the leader of the raid, Ronnie Biggs—just one of his lesser-known accomplices.

At 2:00 p.m., I had my first free period, and I followed a crowd of kids out of the school gates to have a cigarette round the corner. I couldn't quite believe no one stopped me. I stood a little way apart from them and lit up, half-wishing I had the courage to go over and introduce myself and half-thinking that I needed to play it cool. *Don't push anyone off the step.*

A big green car pulled up next to me, and an enormous teenager heaved his massive frame out of the passenger seat. *This is it*, I thought to myself. *I'm going to be beaten to a pulp.*

"Got a fag?" the giant asked me. He had a low, booming voice.

"Sure," I said, flipping open my box, working on my new accent.

"Thanks," he said, accepting a light. "Are you new then?"

"Yeah," I said, desperately trying to speak as little as possible so as not to give the game away. "You?"

"I left," he said. "My name's Neil." Neil was about six-foot-three, and his voice was deep, loud, and slow.

"I'm Tom," I said.

Another guy had gotten out of the car and came to join us. "I'm Robin," he said as he messed around with a rolling paper and a pouch of loose tobacco. He had blond, curly hair and didn't say much.

We stood smoking in the sun for a little bit. "Well, this is fucking boring," said Neil after a while, and he turned to Robin. "Want to go up to the J-Tree?"

"Sure," said Robin. "I've got a little bit of hash."

"Want to come up to the woods with us?" asked Neil.

"Sure," I said as nonchalantly as I could. Were we really about to get into the car and drive off to the woods for a joint while school was still going on? Apparently so. Maybe Oxted County School was going to be okay after all.

Robin's car was an old green Vauxhall Viva. As we drove up into the woods above Oxted, he rolled another cigarette with his right hand, steered with his knees, and shifted the gearstick with his left.

"Oops," he would say every time the car lurched toward the verge.

This seemed to annoy Neil. "Robin, can you just keep your bloody hands on the wheel, please? Here, have one of my cigarettes rather than one of those roll-ups."

Robin took one and slyly smiled.

We made it to the woods and parked under a giant oak tree anchored into the ground with massive, knotted roots, its branches spreading out above us, filtering the afternoon sunshine.

"I'll skin up," said Robin, producing a little block of hash from somewhere inside the car. He began burning it with his lighter and crumbling it into some rolling papers. He pulled out his bag of tobacco and was about to add some when Neil said in an exasperated tone that suggested they had had this conversation before, "Please don't use that disgusting tobacco, Robin. Here, have one of my cigarettes."

I thought I saw Robin do his sly smile again as he reached out for the cigarette without looking up from the papers. These guys could push each other's buttons like an old married couple. Robin licked the cigarette down the seam and pulled it open halfway, spreading the tobacco onto the hash. He rolled up the joint, and we smoked it while sitting on the hood of the car. Robin played a Pat Metheny album on the stereo.

"Please," said Neil, "can you turn this terrible music off?"

"No," said Robin. "It's my car, and the man's a genius."

So I sat there and listened to Pat Metheny in the woods with my new friends Robin and Neil. They asked me what I was doing at the school, and I thought, *Well, what the hell, we're stoned, we're together, we're friends now,* and I told them about Eton.

"Oh, right," said Robin. "You're Tom *Sykes*."

"Yeah?" I said.

"You live next door to my grandma. She told me about you."

Robin's grandma, Molly Delwiche, lived in a tiny, immaculate, Victorian terraced house at the bottom of the driveway of my uncle's house, which we were living in. When Robin came to visit his grandmother, he would come up and knock on my door. He was supposed to be at school, but he wasn't there much. He and the school had lost interest in each other. At Oxted there were few serious attempts to get truants into school if, like Robin, they were over sixteen, the legal school-leaving age. With thirty kids or so in each class—compared with eight or nine at Eton—the teachers had enough on their plates without chasing down missing students.

Robin's dad was an electrician, and his mom was a nurse, and they lived just a few miles away from me in Godstone. For lots of reasons, Robin became one of my closest friends at Oxted. There was the geographical proximity of his grandma to my house, there was the fact that it wasn't too far out of his way to pick me up on the way to the pub on Friday and Saturday nights, and there was the fact we both liked smoking pot. After the pub, we would lumber around the country lanes in his massive, gas-guzzling vehicle and park in out-of-the-way lanes to smoke hash and listen to Robin's eclectic music collection. He was into rare jazz, Frank Zappa, and Funkadelic.

One summer Saturday night, we drove into the countryside after the pub, as usual. We parked by a locked gate at the entrance to a field. We were smoking a joint when a cop car pulled up behind us and flashed its lights twice.

"Oh, shit," we both said simultaneously. We tried to grab the drugs and papers, but a young cop was already banging on the window with a flashlight. The cops found the marijuana, of course, and hauled us down to the police station. There they split us up and strip-searched me. I had to take off all my clothes while I was standing on a plastic sheet. Then the young policeman who had arrested me told me to squat down.

"Why?" I asked. "Do you think I have drugs wedged in my butt cheeks?"

"Just squat, please, Mr. Sykes," he said in a tone that suggested this was more painful for him than it was for me.

After that, they led me to a cell. The cell was just a square room built of unpainted cinder blocks with a metal toilet, a wooden bench built into the wall, and a door with a viewing window.

I sat on the bench. This was the second time I had been in a police cell in my life; the first time was an incident two years previously when I had been caught riding my sister's moped. I felt much less concerned this time around. The law had been gradually shifting toward the decriminalization of cannabis over the past few years, and considering the tiny amount of resin we had on us—less than an eighth of an ounce—we were unlikely to get anything more than a caution. They probably wouldn't even call my mom. Still, I reflected, it wasn't exactly a great place to be.

I lay back on my bench with my hands behind my head and started reading the graffiti. I was only mildly surprised to recognize the names of some of the kids who went to my school. One tag, written over a smiley face, read, "Smiffy woz 'ere!"

After a few hours, the same young policeman came and opened my cell door. I followed him down the passageway to a door marked "Interview Room."

The interview room was painted an unsettling shade of green. He took my fingerprints and then sat me down, at which point another, older, more senior officer came into the room.

The old cop began by asking me a few perfunctory questions, then he leaned across the table and switched the tape recorder off with a dramatic flourish.

"So," the old cop said, puffing up his red cheeks, "where did you get the stuff? Tell us where you got it, and you're out of here, no record."

I was still high, and I tried not to laugh. This guy was playing the part of a cop he had seen on some TV show. They had found less than £10 worth of hash on me. I wasn't exactly looking at jail time.

"Think it's funny, eh?" he said. "Well, let me tell you something. Your friend Robin is over the legal blood alcohol limit, and unless you tell us where you got this stuff, we're going to do him for drunk driving."

Now this was serious. If Robin couldn't drive, how would I get to the pub? I had to do it. I gave them the name. "We got it from a guy called Greg," I said.

The cop nodded. "Greg. Right. Thanks very much. Surname, please."

"I can't give you his surname," I protested.

"Give it to me or your friend Robin gets a breath test," he replied.

I sighed. "Greg Davidson," I said, telling them the truth and making a mental note never to be a spy. "He lives in Redhill."

The officer gave a badly hidden I-told-you-so smile to his junior. "Great. That's it. You can go now, Mr. Sykes."

I stood up and followed the young cop out of the room and down the corridor to the front of the station. Robin was waiting for me there. We looked at each other sheepishly.

The young policeman actually drove us back to Robin's car, although he clearly knew Robin was over the drinking limit. "Mind how you go now," he said as he dropped us off.

The car was unlocked. We got in and sat there in silence for a few moments.

"I can't believe they didn't breath test me," said Robin eventually.

"They said they would unless I told them who we got the dope off," I said. The headlights from a passing car washed over Robin's face. On this little lane, it was probably the policeman heading back to the station, but I couldn't tell.

"Me too," said Robin. We sat in silence for a moment, then we both said simultaneously, "I told them it was Greg."

We looked at each other and then cracked up laughing.

"Well, you know, sod it," I said. "It's true. Why should you lose your license? The guy makes enough money. Occupational hazard."

We knew we had broken the code by grassing Greg up, though, and as Robin drove me home, we justified what we had done.

"He lives in Redhill..."

"He's small-time, they won't go after him..."

"The cop was just playing tough..."

Eventually Robin said, "And I only gave them his first name. I mean, there must be loads of people called Greg dealing pot round here."

I went silent for a bit. Then I said, "I gave them the last name too."

Another silence. Then I said, "Oops."

We thought for a beat. "Well, he's fucked then," Robin said, and we both collapsed into stoned giggles again.

## −4,553 DAYS

During the summer of 1992, the year after I was expelled from Eton, things started to really improve for the first time since my dad left. We moved out of my uncle's house, and my mom bought her own house in Oxted, the town where I went to school. It was on the side of a major road, next door to one of Oxted's roughest pubs, the Wheatsheaf, and very oddly designed. When you walked in the front door off the street, you were confronted with two impossibly steep staircases—one going up to two bedrooms and one going down to the kitchen, sitting room, and garden. It was much, much smaller than the cottage my uncle had lent us, which I then realized was not a cottage at all but a substantial country residence.

One thing that our new house did have going for it was that by a strange quirk, the garden ran into about two acres of woodland that was technically owned by the local council but effectively part of our garden. It had a little river running through it, and my uncle had allowed me to disassemble an old chicken shed that was in the garden of the cottage and take it to Riverside—as our new house was optimistically called.

The reason my uncle had let me take the shed with us was because I had kitted it out with armchairs, sofas, and a stereo. When the shed relocated with us to Oxted, my popularity exploded. The new house, as well as being next door to the Wheatsheaf, was just down the road from the Crown, the pub we all used to drink in.

The heart and soul of the shed crew was me; Robin; Neil; Simon, a computer whiz kid; and Steve, a budding hippie with a ponytail. We kitted it out with armchairs, hooked up an extension cord all the way up the garden to the house, and put a barbecue outside.

We would meet at the shed most nights to get stoned. My mother did not turn a blind eye to the pot so much as she just never saw it. She didn't know what to look for. She hardly ever drank—alcohol made her feel sick—and had never taken drugs. Poachers make the best gamekeepers, but my mom was blissfully ignorant.

Mentally, Mom was now much better than when my dad had left. She had thrown away all her antidepressants, and her new drug of choice seemed to be painting the staircase different colors. At least once a fortnight, during the painting mania, I would come home, put the key in the front door, and find it was bolted. So I would have to walk around the back way, climb over the fence to the shed, and walk up the garden to find my mom, paintbrush in hand, brewing incredibly strong coffee and painting the hallway and stairs silver, lavender, or green.

Every month or so, however, terrible migraines would strike her down for five or six days on end. Fred, who was nine, and Josh, who was four, would silently tiptoe around the house, filled with foreboding. I would cook eggs for them—all my sisters had left home for university and careers by now—and sometimes invite them to the shed in the evenings, where they would join my friends and cook sausages over the crackling fire on the sharpened ends of sticks. They were too small to ask too many questions about the "funny cigarettes" we made.

So my mom wasn't really doing the teenage drug watch thing. "I was just happy you were making friends after you were expelled from that awful school," she told me years later, when I asked her about it. "I thought it was lovely that everyone would come round and see you. I really had no idea about the drugs. And I thought the drinking and being sick was, well, just pure *naughtiness*. It's what boys do."

It was true that my friends loved coming round to my house. Mom, who had her hair stained bright red with henna, would make us coffee and flapjacks when we got the munchies. Fred would carry them down to the shed on a tray. She was always trying to make my friends eat yogurt and pumpkin seeds. Her personal health strategy revolves around the production and consumption of vast amounts of homemade yogurt. Her belief in yogurt as a universal panacea is so powerful that she still can't let someone step through the door without forcefully offering them a bowlful.

In the shed, we were pursuing our own route to enlightenment with the aid of LSD. We bought tabs for a few pounds each, and then we would wander around Oxted tripping our heads off for several hours before heading back to the shed to listen to music and smoke pot—which we still sometimes bought from Greg, the guy I had grassed up but who, weirdly enough and to my great relief, never got busted.

I loved acid, but the intensity of the experience always scared me. My visions would morph dangerously toward the nightmarish if I shut my eyes for too long. I spent most of my time waiting to come down. Then Steve and Neil took a trip and had communal visions that the trees were getting up and walking around on their roots, chasing them, coming to get them. Neil quit all drugs as a result. Steve was not so easily put off.

Their bad trip scared me, but I reassured myself that they had made mistakes. They had taken too many trips, mixed halves and quarters of different brands, asked for trouble.

Still, I never kidded myself that acid was safe, and my bad trip came at the famous Glastonbury music festival—a three-day jamboree of music, drugs, and lentil-eating hippies in the West Country. The festival took place right after the end of term, and I was on a bender to celebrate the fact that I had finished school. I had sworn off drugs and alcohol for two months before my exams, and I suspected I would do well enough, when the results came through, to get into Edinburgh University in Scotland.

So Glastonbury was a real party. It was gorgeous weather. We had been tripping all day, wandering around the festival and laughing hysterically at the various sideshow freaks. I sat down to have a cup of coffee with Steve several hours after the trip had worn off. With no warning at all, I went into convulsions.

Suddenly I was seven feet above the ground looking down on myself. My head was thrown way back, and I could only see the whites of my eyes. I looked like I was having a fit.

From my vantage point up in the sky, I could see all around. My mind was very clear. I was dying; there was absolutely no doubt about it. I rose up, higher and higher in the sky, ten feet, twenty feet, maybe more. My head remained the center of my vision. I could see the paper coffee cup on the table, even the stand where I had bought my coffee. Thousands of festivalgoers were milling around me. To my left sat my friend Steve. He had grabbed my arm and was shaking me, shouting something I couldn't hear. I was up there for several seconds before I noticed that the other guy sitting at our table was this boy, Matthew Mole, who I didn't actually like that much. He'd been following our group around for about a year now.

*In fact,* I thought, outraged, *he's a pain in the ass, that guy.* There was no way I was going to die with Matthew Mole sitting next to me. He'd be dining out on this anecdote for years.

I was panicking. I had to get out of this. I tried to dive down, and suddenly I was plummeting, and then I was back, back in my body again. My eyes rolled forward in their sockets, and I could hear what Steve was screaming: "FUCK, TOM, FUCK, FUCK, FUCK."

I looked at him, swiveled my head a few degrees to the right, and shot a stream of projectile vomit out of my mouth.

I'll never forget the extraordinary sound of a hundred-plus people simultaneously shouting, "URRGGH," as the puke either hit them or flew past their faces.

Steve was screaming, "TOM, TOM, ARE YOU ALL RIGHT? ANSWER ME. ARE YOU ALL RIGHT?"

I was. I felt a thousand percent sober. I looked at him with wide eyes. "I'm fine, man," I said. "You won't believe what just happened to me."

I never took acid again.

## −4,222 DAYS

Instead I switched to Ecstasy.

Ecstasy was sweeping the UK when I began taking it in 1992. It cost £25 a pop, and the pills were huge, purple lozenges—horse pills, we used to joke. We would go to the rave clubs in the East End of London with our pills hidden in our shoes or underwear to get past the bouncers. As soon as we got inside, we would pop them, washing them down with a bottle of water. The first thirty minutes were usually spent trying to work out whether or not the pills were duds.

"Are you feeling anything yet?" we would ask each other incessantly.

Then suddenly, a warm feeling would start to tingle in your stomach, followed swiftly by an overwhelming urge to take a crap that should not on any account be acted on.

Then the beat would kick in.

Club UK was an enormous venue that could accommodate two-thousand-plus clubbers in four or five different rooms. Each room played a different kind of music.

Ecstasy has many remarkable effects. The first is that even banal house music sounds insanely good. The bass pumps through you, reverberating in your chest, and you start to dance. Even if you're a middle-class, white, English public school boy pretending to be tough, you feel cool. You can't help it—your hands are in the air; there's a stupid grin on your face. The lights start moving faster and faster, and suddenly you get it. You get the whole dancing thing, and you're one with the music. Then you realize that the whole club, the whole *world* actually, is dancing along with you.

As serotonin floods your brain, you feel happy, happier than you have ever felt before in your life. Sweaty football hooligans with shaved heads come up to you and say, "I love you, man!" and you hug. Girls, pretty girls, beautiful girls with deep, dark eyes and skin shining with sweat are dancing with you. Then you're kissing them, and they are kissing you, slimy and gorgeous and damp, the texture of tongue, then you are both dancing together, laughing, laughing, laughing.

As the pills wear off and the club empties, you get in your friend's car and drive home, smoking a joint and talking about the night, listening to more tunes on a pirate radio station as the sun is coming up, flocks of pigeons swooping low over the streets and blowing your mind. You get home, make some tea, and smoke some more joints, maybe outside in the early morning sunshine. Then you climb into bed and sleep for a few hours.

When you wake up, you are still a bit high. You have another joint to set the reaction off again. You listen to some music, then maybe head to the pub to have a few Sunday-night pints and meet up with your group of mates, all the time talking and laughing about the night before.

Ecstasy was the perfect drug for the United Kingdom. The active ingredient, MDMA, swamps the brain with dopamine and chemically obliges even the most uptight and reserved Brits to express their love to complete strangers. Football violence, where British men have traditionally unloaded their feelings by staving in a rival supporter's head with a beer bottle, dropped dramatically for three or four years when Ecstasy was at the height of its popularity. There were even reports of hooligans popping pills halfway through a game, and at the end, the losing side would hug the winners, saying, "You deserved it, man."

By the time I got to Edinburgh University the following year, E was becoming cheaper and cheaper—as little as a pound a pill. But something else happened as well. The highs were not as good. We began needing to take two or three pills to get the same effect. It became less and less uncommon to hear of people taking six, nine, or twelve pills in a night. I don't know whether the pills were not as good or if our brains just burned out somewhere along the line.

We had all believed Ecstasy was nonaddictive and harmless—a safe, happy high—but then regular Ecstasy users began to get chronically depressed. You'd take it on a Sunday and feel blue till Wednesday. Scientists postulated that, because of the chemical assistance, our brains had forgotten how to feel happy naturally.

Then people started dying. Every week, one or two people would drop dead in the clubs, usually of heat exhaustion from dancing so hard. Did that stop us? Not likely—we just drank loads of water while we were E-ing instead.

The turning point in the received wisdom on Ecstasy came when the media latched onto the story of a girl named Leah Betts, who died while she was taking the drug. Pictures of her last hours in hospital, her face bloated and bruised beyond recognition, were used in antidrug campaigns. Around that time, I decided Ecstasy was dangerous and had to be treated with respect, not munched like candy.

So I would never take more than two; I made sure I drank plenty of water; and I always, always went to bed at the end of the night.

I knew what I was doing. I had a system. I had it under control. I'd be just fine.

## −4090 DAYS

Edinburgh was just like me—it was either getting drunk or in the throes of a ruinous hangover. Most people choose their university on the basis of where they are likely to get the best education in their chosen subject, along with other considerations such as where their friends are going or the cost of living. My major consideration in choosing Edinburgh University was Scottish licensing laws. In England, the pubs closed at eleven—not nearly enough time to get properly drunk—but Edinburgh was different. The pubs were open late.

There was a famous pub called the Phoenix just around the corner from where I lived on Broughton Street. It was open till two in the morning and reopened at six in the morning as an "early morning house." The official line was that this was so postal workers could have a few pints after they came off the night shift. The reality, at 6:00 a.m., was a bar six deep with students, clubbers, and alcoholics fighting for a drink to keep their buzz on from the night before. Oasis and Blur blared out of the jukebox, and marijuana smoke billowed out of the booths. I went back to visit a few years after I had left university and asked John the landlord if they were still open that early. "Och, no," he said, shaking his head. "It just got too feckin' busy. We dinnae open till eight now."

The Phoenix was a magical place for me and my friends. It wasn't run-down in the slightest, but it was simple, straightforward, and unpretentious. The floor was covered in brown carpets, the booths were brown leather, and the room was dominated by an enormous oak bar. They sold pints for £1.50 and toasted sandwiches for 90P. I ate there. I drank there. I cashed my cheques there. I even took my future wife there on our first date.

I met Sasha on Valentine's Day 1997. I was twenty-two, in my last year at university, and we were both taking part in a blind-date game organized by some friends of mine every year for singletons on Valentine's Day. I had seen Sasha a few times before, when I had been delivering hash to a friend of hers, and I got my friends to rig the dating lottery so I could take her out. I was told to meet her at the corner of Broughton Street. So that we could recognize each other, I was told to smoke a cigar, and she would be drinking a can of lager.

About twenty minutes later, I spied Sasha walking up Broughton Street. The first thing I noticed about her was that she was shorter than I—about five foot seven—and had long, blonde hair and massive boobs. She was wearing flared jeans and carrying a strappy bag over her shoulder. Her can of lager was empty. I tossed my cigar, leapt over the fence to greet her, and kissed her hello. Then I took her to the Phoenix for a drink. Who said chivalry is dead?

Sasha sat on a leather bench, and I sat on a stool with a view of the bar, which meant I could just flick my hand at the bartender, and he would bring another two pints. Sasha is Irish, and we drank Guinness. The barman ran me a tab, and we quickly lost count of how much we drank. I deliberately set out to get her as drunk as possible so I could get her to come home with me.

Things went well. Sasha was studying to be an architect, and I wanted to be a writer, and we seemed to connect on every level. I was fascinated by her Irishness—it seemed rare and exotic to me—and she was intrigued by my story of being expelled from Eton. Before we knew it, it was two o'clock, and the pub was closing. We walked along the street, amorous from the Guinness, heading back to my house.

Much later that night, Sasha was in my bedroom. I peeled off her clothes while she lay in my bed. Her skin was pale white. Her boobs were every bit as fabulous as her clothed figure suggested. Just as I started to get my own clothes off, she suddenly yelped, grabbed the duvet, and ran out of my room. I was puzzled and drunkenly surrendered to sleep.

When I woke up, she was gone, and I had no idea what had happened. A few days later, when I rang and asked her to go out with me again, she said yes. I was delighted. Finally I had found a girl who could drink as much as I could. This had to be the perfect woman.

My best friend at university was Olly Taylor. We lived together for the whole four years of college, spending the last two years in a huge apartment on Leith Walk. It had eighteen-foot ceilings and wood floors and was owned by my friend Nick. It was perfect because it was just around the corner from the Phoenix, and we only had to pay £50 a week in rent.

University was supposed to shape our minds, but most of us set about assiduously frying them instead. Most nights Olly, Nick, and I would head out to the pub at about ten and drink until one or two in the morning. Then, back home, Olly and I would listen to some music and finally crash out about three. I would wake at ten or eleven in the morning, except on Fridays, when I had a tutorial at nine.

A few of my close friends actually lost their minds altogether. One stopped smoking marijuana in the last year at Edinburgh because it gave him such severe panic attacks. Another friend did so much acid that he had to be sectioned in an asylum after breaking into the landlady's bedroom in a pub and getting into her bed.

In our first year, Olly and I shared an apartment with two girls. One of them got pregnant but didn't tell anyone. When she had the baby in secret, it died, and she hid the body in the freezer of her apartment in London. We only found out what had happened when swarms of newspaper reporters descended on the university, offering anyone who knew her tens of thousands of pounds for photographs of her with her boyfriend. The only heartwarming thing about the whole saga was that everyone told the reporters to get lost.

I walked around in a daze for weeks afterward, wondering how such a thing could have happened under my nose. Had she been pregnant when we were living with her? Why hadn't she asked us for help? Surely it didn't have anything to do with the joints, the Es, and the three bottles of wine we shared every night?

The drug- and alcohol-fueled insanity at Edinburgh made me look sane, normal, even boring. All I did was drink a lot, smoke a lot of pot, and take speed or Ecstasy on the weekend (I could only afford cocaine very occasionally). *I* was fine. *I* had never been sectioned. *I* didn't have any bodies in the ice compartment.

But still, I was aware something was happening. When I went to Edinburgh, I was a social drinker—a heavy one, given to frequent binges, but definitely a social drinker. I could go a few days without alcohol, and when I wanted to stop, I would go home to bed. But somehow, by the time I left, I had lost control. I would wake up in the mornings suffering memory loss, wondering what I had done the night before, nervous about finding out the answer, ashamed. Somewhere during those four years of indulgence, I stepped off the ledge and into the deep water. I spent a lot of time later in my life trying to work out just where that point was.

It might have been when my sister Plum called me and told me she was worried about me. She'd heard tales about my drinking, even though she was living several thousand miles away in New York, where she had been hired by American *Vogue*. I agreed with her that

I should quit drinking for six months. I was dry for about six hours.

Maybe I scrambled the eggs when my tutor, whom I saw every Friday at nine, asked me to stay behind at the end of class. When it was just us left in the room, he shut the door and asked me whether I had a problem with drinking, as I had never showed up to his class on time and/or not smelling of booze.

"No, no," I said. "It's just the class starts so early."

"Nine is not early, Tom," he said, "unless you've been out till three in the morning the night before."

I left his class determined to *do something* about my problem. What I *did* was circle around the student health center, toying with the idea of going in and saying, "I'm an addict." Then I thought, *I'm fine*, walked home, skinned up a giant joint, put on a Funkadelic CD, and got into bed for the rest of the day.

Or maybe the moment I broke the tape was when I ran to the bathroom at the Phoenix, threw up, and came back to the bar to order another pint.

In the end, of course, it doesn't really matter when I became an alcoholic. One moment I reached down, and the sand was there; the next time I tried, I couldn't touch the bottom anymore. Once you are in the deep water, the current gets stronger faster. It sucks you farther and farther out, out to a place where you can't really see the land and the people walking around on the beach and building sand-castles anymore. All you see is other people who have been caught by the tide. Some of the people are even farther out than you are. And you say to yourself, *Well, I could swim back anytime I like. But maybe I'll give it another hour or so. It's fun out here. The beach looks kind of boring anyway.*

## −2,624 DAYS

I didn't quit drinking for my final exams at Edinburgh, but I did stop smoking pot for three months. The transformation was quite incredible. I could remember things. I could focus for more than twenty minutes at a time. I only had to read a paragraph once to make sense of it. I crammed four years' worth of work into those twelve weeks. After I took my last exam, I celebrated by buying an ounce bag of grass from my dealer, James.

I moved down to London, where I rented a disgusting apartment above a kebab shop with my friends Olly and Tom Craig. I managed to get an appointment to see Stephen Clackson, the news editor of the London commuter paper the *Evening Standard*. We met in the work cafeteria, which was located in the vast, glass-covered atrium of Associated Newspapers, just off Kensington High Street, where he chain-smoked Gauloises cigarettes while I showed him my cuttings book. It had about ten pieces I had written for various university publications carefully glued into it. He started leafing through them, then his cell phone went off, and he was summoned back to the office.

"Look, I've got to go," he said, scooping my cuttings book under his arm. "But I'll take a look at these later."

"Oh," I said, freaking out because he was about to disappear with my only asset in my quest for a job in journalism. "Couldn't I copy them for you or something?"

He paused, looked at me sternly, and said, "I'm not going to lose them."

"Oh, erm, okay," I conceded, but Mr. Clackson was already streaking across the marble floor to the glass elevator.

One week passed. I heard nothing from Mr. Clackson. Two weeks. Still nothing. In the third week, I finally called the *Standard*.

"News desk," a woman's voice said when I called.

"Oh, hello," I started nervously. "Is Stephen Clackson there, please?"

"He's busy," said the woman, sounding impatient. "What's it about?"

"I came in to see Mr. Clackson about a job, and I gave him my cuttings book. He said he would return it, but I haven't heard anything yet," I said.

"Why didn't you give him a copy?" she asked.

"Well, he took the originals," I said, feeling stupid, "and the thing is, I don't care if you can't give me a job. I just need the cuttings back. . . ."

"Hold on," the woman said.

The line went silent, clicked, rang again, and I heard Mr. Clackson's cool, calm, collected voice say, "Mr. Sykes. And how are you, young man?"

"Er, not bad," I said. "The only thing is . . . "

"I know," he interrupted. "Your cuttings. They seem to have gotten lost. Why don't you come in for a couple of weeks and see if you can find them?"

"Oh, okay, great, thanks," I said, totally flustered.

"I'll put you with my secretary, Karen Douglas."

The line went silent again, for longer this time, then clicked back to the woman I had been speaking to before.

"Hello, Tom," she said, sounding much friendlier. "Nine thirty on Monday okay?"

"Er, great," I said.

"See you then," she replied and hung up.

And that's how I got my start in journalism. It turned out I could write, and my two weeks turned into a year.

I loved the *Standard*, not least because it was a drinkers' newspaper, and it was largely staffed by drunks. The first edition went out at 7:30 a.m., with a hangover and hair of the dog, and the last at about 4:00 p.m., with updates phoned in from the pub where we gathered every afternoon to gossip, bitch, and drink away the day. One of the few exceptions was Clackson himself, who drank precisely one glass of wine a day at lunch and got to the office at 5:45 every morning.

Drinking was part of the job description on Fleet Street, as the national press is known by newspapermen in the UK (regardless of the fact that all the British newspapers had moved out of the actual London street of that name long before I started). I embraced the booze culture of news wholeheartedly. The famous drinkers at the *Standard* were mainly men in their late forties or early fifties, hardened hacks like Colin Adamson or Richard Holliday, masters at turning around copy from a murder scene or an abduction in a matter of minutes and filing on the spot—or, more frequently, from the nearest licensed purveyor of intoxicating liquor. Gervaise "Barmy" Webb was another fixture at the local bar, Jimmy's, where he had an understanding with the bar staff that whenever he saw a cockroach, he would dance a little jig to distract the customers in return for preferential, sometimes complimentary service. Barmy—as his name suggested—was such a strange guy that his suddenly breaking out into a two-step hardly seemed unusual.

Another pub we frequented, tucked away behind Kensington Church Road, was the Elephant. Every opportunity I got, I would head to the Elephant, whose wood-paneled walls were adorned with famous front pages from the newspaper's history, for a session with Barmy, Colin, or Richard, the *Standard*'s very own holy trinity of inebriation. I wanted what they had—a front page every week and a well-lubricated, first-name relationship with every bargirl for three square miles.

Colin—a tough, no-nonsense Scotsman who suffered terribly from eczema—was a particularly prodigious drinker. He rolled into the office one day after lunch, saying, "God, I'm plastered. I've had three pints."

I was confused. "Three pints, Colin? That doesn't seem very much."

"Aye—but they were pints o' wine," he replied and sat down heavily in front of his screen to light one of the forty cigarettes he smoked daily and make his final adds to the front page of the last edition.

But the tides of change were running the other way. The *Standard*'s drinking culture was dying out. The management was becoming less and less tolerant of the drunk gang, and increasing numbers of the new guard of reporters were earnest, swotty, and square. They sat at their screens all day, typing furiously, and never had hangovers in the morning. I pitied them their serious, joyless existence and determined never to be like them. Even when I crawled into the office at five thirty, head pounding from another late night at the Elephant or Jimmy's, I held their sober lifestyles in contempt. After all, I could get through the day just fine, and I was getting more stories in the paper than they were, anyway.

I wasn't particularly popular at the *Standard*. The fact that I had simply waltzed into my job without paying my dues at the coalface of local journalism irritated a lot of the old-school, working-class journalists who had done just that. I looked faintly like Clackson, too, so the other staff joked I was his secret love child, and that was why I had been given the job.

E-mail was still only a fledgling technology in our office in 1997, so we communicated using "onscreen interoffice memos." It was easy to find out what other people had messaged about you. I could never resist. One message that I remember said, "If that Tom pillock sits opposite me for much longer, he will find himself with considerably less space between his ears than he has at present."

But the pub had a magical bonding effect. The moment I sat down at a table in the Elephant with Colin, Richard, or Barmy, I was part of the club; we all got along, united by beer, whiskey, and vodka and tonics.

I loved hearing the drinking stories. Colin told me how he used to sleep all night on the barroom floor at Harvey's on Fleet Street, then go straight to work. Richard told me about drinking the East European liquor Slivovitch in a bunker while under Bosnian Serb mortar fire. "After a few hits of that, you're like, 'Come on then, you bastards, give us your best shot,' " explained Richard, standing in the middle of the pub and waggling his ass in the air.

My big break at the *Standard* came in a great disguise. A Swedish company had come out with tights for men. I posed in them, à la Christine Keeler, sitting backward on a chair, and wrote eight hundred words to go with it.

The features editor, Nicola Jeal, loved my piece; and she gave me more and more work. The piece on the tights was even used as part of the *Standard*'s ad campaign. Although I wasn't too happy about being plastered on bus stops and subway stations all over London in my tights, I was chuffed with the tagline, "The Best Writers Are in the *Evening Standard*." So I couldn't take public transport for a few months. So what? I was getting somewhere.

The best thing about all this success was that I was earning a fortune. In a good week, I could make over £1,000. I spent most of it in the pub, but I was spending more and more of my cash buying drugs—marijuana and, increasingly, cocaine—from my dealer, James.

I had first met James when I lived in Edinburgh, where he was also a student, studying geography, and I used to buy weed from him. When I finished university and moved to London, James moved too. He lived in a musty, sparsely furnished house in south London; and several nights a week, I would drive over there in my beat-up Fiat Panda, which Plum had given me, to score.

Over the years, James had become much more than just a dealer—he had become one of my best friends. On the afternoons I didn't go to the pub, I would race up to his house and sit in his garden smoking joints and waiting for the rest of our friends to finish work. We would spend hours smoking weed and throwing little twigs into the spiders' webs that covered his garden, watching with fascination as the spiders pounced on the twigs, cut them out of the webs so they fell to the ground, and then swiftly patched up their insect traps and returned to the center to wait for lunch.

The reason James became one of my best friends was basically because he was one of the few people who liked to smoke as much as I did, and he always had some hash or skunk (superstrong grass grown under artificial lights) on him. Cocaine was great if I had the money, because it meant I could drink all night without blacking out. If I didn't have the cash, well, James usually had a package on him that he would let me dip into for free.

## −2,013 DAYS

Sasha was a bit younger than I was, so she had stayed at Edinburgh after I left. We split up and hardly had any contact. The following year, she came to London from Dublin, where she was living, on her way to Greece, where she was going for a month to visit a friend.

Sasha had chopped her long hair off and was wearing a skirt over her jeans. She looked gorgeous, and I fell right back in love with her. Before the end of the night, I had agreed to visit her for ten days in Greece to coincide with my twenty-fifth birthday. I had several weeks of holiday time from the *Standard* that I wanted to use up, so the trip made perfect sense.

And so it was that I woke up the day after my birthday in a cheap but clean hotel on the Greek island of Paxos, with last night's ouzo banging noxiously around my head and a faint smell of charred bacon in the air. My eyes hardly open, I reached out my hand, grabbed the bottle of water by our bed, and took a gulp. Something solid hit my tongue, and I sprayed water all over the room in disgust. I knew instantly what it was. The soaked, decomposing cigarette butt lay on the floor, and I groaned in disgust.

Sasha opened her eyes.

"What is it?" she asked.

"There was a fag butt in the water, and I just took a gulp," I said.

"Eughh. You poor thing," said Sasha.

We lay there a few minutes. "We've got to get up," I said. "We've got to check out of here by twelve."

"What time is it now?"

I checked my watch. "Eleven. How you feeling?"

"Uggh," said Sasha in reply. "What did we do last night?"

"I don't know. I remember being in that bar drinking ouzo, then I think I had an argument with the barman about the bill. I can't really remember after that."

We lay back in silence for a few moments more. A bell clanged arrhythmically near our room as a goat outside munched grass. Fucking goats.

"Come on then," I said, hauling myself into a sitting position on the edge of the bed. "Let's do it."

We must have been halfway through packing our stuff when Sasha started pulling the twisted sheet straight on the bed.

"You don't have to make the bed," I said, irritated at the delay. "We're leaving, aren't we . . . *shit*."

We were both staring at the bedsheet, which had two big, black-edged holes burnt through it.

"Shit," I said again. The blood was pumping to my head. So that's what the burning smell was. I must have fallen asleep with a lit cigarette. We were lucky to be alive.

"Oh, my God, Tommy, this really is not funny," said Sasha, sitting down heavily on the bed again. She rifled through the rumpled sheets and plucked out a half-burned cigarette. Thank God it had gone out.

"You really can't smoke in bed when you are so pissed," Sasha said. She reached out for her socks and was just about to put them on when she stopped and said, "What's that?"

I sat down next to her on the bed. Sasha had a huge, angry blister on her shin. It looked like a burn.

"It looks like a burn," she said.

"Oh, my God. I am so sorry," I said.

"I can't believe you got so pissed you burnt a hole in my leg as well as nearly burning up the bed," said Sasha, her eyes bright with tears.

"It was an accident!" I said.

I got up and stalked angrily to the bathroom. I looked at myself in the mirror. *You idiot,* I thought. I shouted through to the other room, "Anyway, you're no better. I can't believe you were so pissed you didn't wake up although your leg was on fire."

I showered in pained silence. I dried off and went back to the bedroom. Sasha was sitting on the bed looking dumbly at the blister.

"I'm sorry, Monkey," I whispered as I kissed her gently. "Really, I am so sorry."

"That's okay," sighed Sasha. "I guess you're right. It's my fault as well."

"I've branded you," I tried. "You're mine forever now."

## −1,631 DAYS

In 1998, I joined the *Daily Telegraph* as a trainee; but by the end of 1999, it was clear they weren't going to give me a full-time job. I had argued with the news desk too often, and then there was the time there was a flu bug going around and I called in sick for a week, used the time to get stoned and paint my room above the kebab shop yellow, and then actually did get sick the following week. Also, I was annoyed that, after the success I had had at the *Standard*, I wasn't being given more feature-writing opportunities. I went back to the *Standard* in 2000, age twenty-six, as a fully paid-up member of the staff.

But what was I going to write about? The news desk handed out general assignments, but to really shine, reporters had to develop a specialty topic.

I sounded out Colin and Richard over a few beers at the Elephant one afternoon.

"Write what you know," they both said. What did I like doing?

What did I know? I knew drugs and alcohol. What did I like doing? I liked partying and going out.

"So there's your answer," said Colin. I was going to write about London's youth culture in all its varied forms. I was going to stay out late and cover the party beat.

My first big assignment was to cover the Glastonbury festival in Somerset for the paper—the scene of my acid-fueled, out-of-body teenage experience.

I picked up my pass from Karen at the news desk. When I opened the official-looking envelope, I realized with delight that I had been given an extra guest pass for a friend. It was a no-brainer who I would take. It had to be James, who, in return for a free ticket, would sort me out with all the E, coke, and weed I required.

I rang him and proposed the deal.

"Yeah, sure," said James. "What time do we leave?" Another great thing about James was that, because he never had to go to work, he was always available for impetuous, last-minute road trips.

Driving up to Glastonbury, James stashed his drugs all around the car that the *Standard* had rented me. We had seven grams of coke, fifteen pills, and an ounce of hash, which James hid down various seat backs and ventilation slots. He needn't have bothered. We showed our media passes, and they let us drive in without a search.

The festival began on a Friday. There was no paper on the weekends, as the *Standard* was strictly a commuter title. That meant all I would have to do was file a round-up story on Sunday night for Monday morning. I swore to myself I wouldn't get too wasted before then.

I popped a pill or two on Friday and Saturday nights—nothing too excessive—and on Sunday, I stayed sober while David Bowie played the main stage. I wrote my report of the weekend and called the news desk to phone it in.

"Good job. Thanks, Tom," the night editor said when I had finished. I felt a surge of relief that I had done my job. Now I could get down to the serious business of getting bombed.

I found James dancing to a sound system playing trance outside a blanket stall called Joe Bananas.

"I'm done," I shouted in his ear. "Give us a pill."

James bounced up and down on the spot, wrapped in a blanket. "I can't, mate. I've got rid of them all," he said.

I looked at him in shocked amazement, then exploded.

"YOU WHAT?" I screamed at him. "You fucking cunt. I can't believe I brought you here, got you in and everything, and you didn't even save one fucking pill for me."

"Sorry, mate," he said. "I sold the last one for five quid to get some cash to buy a hot dog."

"To buy a fucking hot dog?" I shouted, panicking badly. "There's free fucking hot dogs in the press tent, you wanker. Stop fucking dancing."

James was reaching down into his shoe. He pulled out a little plastic bag with three pills in it. He was grinning at me.

"Tommy, Tommy," he laughed, waving the bag in front of my face. "I'm only joking, mate. Course I saved some for tonight. I'm only winding you up. Ha ha ha!"

I felt the relief surge over me. I hugged James, and he hugged me back. "You bastard," I said. He took one of the pills out and handed it to me, mimicking me, saying, " 'A fucking hot dog!' "

I smiled at him and then looked at the pill in my hand. It looked like one of those tiny mints they give you tins of for free in the smarter hotels, but thicker, with rough, crumbly edges. I tapped a guy on the shoulder who was dancing next to me with a bottle of water.

"Can I borrow your water, mate?" I asked, making the drinking sign. He nodded and passed me the bottle. I washed the pill down with a glug of liquid.

Just before I came up, I thought fleetingly about how pathetically grateful I was that James had actually saved a few pills for me. If he hadn't had them, my whole weekend would have been ruined. And he knew it. I hated it when James played these power games with drugs. He did it with a smile on his face, and it was all a big joke, but it was totally fucked up. He wanted me to be grateful. He wanted to see me lose it or beg, *beg* for the drugs. He was a . . .

The soundtrack of complaints in my head stopped as the pill kicked in. I shut my eyes and rolled them back in my head. I ran my hand through my hair, and it felt like straw. That was a sure sign I was coming up.

The DJ was playing a classic tune called "Sabres of Paradise." The keyboards sounded like searchlights in my ears. The crowd threw its hands in the air, and everyone was dancing with me. I started feeling sick, but I knew to ignore it. I threw up, but my puke looked and tasted like gold. Then I was dancing. "Put your hands in the air," yelled the DJ. I hugged James. "I love you, man. These pills are wicked. I love you, man."

At four in the morning, James and I were finally coming down. We were sitting on the grass around a fire somewhere at the top of the Glastonbury site, and we were smoking joints and drinking beers. I had just spent half an hour chatting to a man whose face was covered in thick, werewolflike hair. I was so wasted, I had asked him about it without any reservations, and he had told me he was from a family of Gypsies. In Eastern Europe, where they'd originally come from, the family was feared and revered as supernatural beings.

James and I kept wandering from one fire to the next, sitting down for a bit, skinning up, and smoking joints. The smoke felt amazing in my lungs, clear, purifying.

"Amazing pills, man," I said, for maybe the thirty-fourth time.

"Tommy, would I ever let you down?" grinned James. Then he did his impression of me that he'd been doing all night. " 'A fucking hot dog.' "

"Shut up, you wanker," I said.

We started talking to some hippies who had been attracted by the smell of grass and were desperate for a hit on our joint. James and I teased them, skinning up and passing the joint back and forth between ourselves while the hippies kept trying to be smart and funny and ingratiating in the hope we would give them a hit. We didn't. The power games you could play with drugs were fun when you were holding.

At five, as we sat there wild-eyed, smoking pot, still buzzing from the E, James got out his coke. I was in the middle of taking a sniff when my cell phone rang. I pulled it out in horror and stared at it.

"Who is that?" James asked.

I knew who it was. I flipped open the phone. Before I could speak, Karen was barking down my ear, "Hello, Tom, could you hold while I put you over to Clackson? Thanks."

Shit, shit, shit.

Clackson came on the line. "Hello, Mr. Sykes. Sorry to wake you so early, young man, but I need you to renose your Glasto copy." He was talking very fast and sounded very, very sober. His voice sounded like it was coming from a million miles away.

"Sure," I said, gesturing madly at James and the hippies to shut up. "What do you need?"

Clackson sounded annoyed that I had to ask. "You know, Tom. The usual. What's going on now. What can you actually *see* right now?"

What I could see was James waving a massive joint under my nose and shrugging at me as a crowd of hippies berated him for a hit on it, like a scene out of *Dawn of the Dead*.

"Erm, well," I said. "I don't know, erm, just lots of people packing up to leave and . . ."

Clackson cut me off. "Just file, okay?"

The line went dead. I sat in the grass scribbling on a bit of old napkin with a pencil I found in my pocket. All the hippies kept coming up and asking, "What are you writing, man? What's going on?"

I shouted over to James that we had to find somewhere quieter, that I had to rewrite the first few paragraphs. We got up and ran across the field, trying to find a quiet spot. It was like being stuck in a computer game designed by MC Escher. Everywhere we went was the same, just people trekking through the mud. Eventually I sat down on the grass and tried not to cry.

"James, just try and keep these people away from me for ten minutes, okay? Please?"

I sat down and started to write. As I cobbled together a few lines, James stood over me in the breaking dawn, fending off inquiries from curious, stoned passersby who were all wanting to know what I was doing. After fifteen minutes, he just pretended to be crazy and violent and shouted at anyone who came near, "Just fuck off, okay?" like some obscene—but highly efficient—talking guard dog. *It's only a matter of time before he starts barking,* I thought.

Just as I got the sentences together, the desk rang again.

"Hold for Stephen, please," said Karen.

She put me through. "Okay, ready to go?" asked Clackson.

"Sure," I said as confidently as I could. "Do you want to patch me through to copy?"

"No, we're out of time. I'll take it."

Oh, shit. This was bad. My throat was dry and my voice cracking as I read my pitiful sentences. I heard his keyboard clacking down the line, and then halfway through, the keyboard sound just stopped. When I finished, Clackson waited. And waited. And waited.

"Is that it?" he asked finally.

"Erm, yeah," I said.

"What's going on, Tom?" he asked. "This isn't difficult."

"Sorry, I think I must be sleepy. Just got up."

"You just got up?" he said. "Really?"

"Erm, well, yeah, I haven't actually been to bed yet."

*Oh, Christ. Why did I say that?* Another long pause.

"Tom," said Clackson, "I'll do this for you. Get some sleep and call when you wake up." The phone went dead. My face was white.

James was in hysterics. "I can't believe you just had to file. Look at the state of you."

I couldn't say anything. I wanted to cry. Was I going to be fired? I looked at James and I hated him. Hated his drugs. Hated the way he had tricked me into taking them. Fucking dealer cunt.

"Skin up," I said.

And so James and I sat there in the dawn's early light surveying the wreckage of the festival, smoking joint after joint after joint.

The thing I liked about smoking dope was that it just made everything bad go away. So Clackson was a little pissed with me. So what? What did they expect? It was Glastonbury. I was twenty-six. This was what journalists were *supposed* to do, wasn't it? This was the whole point.

Later that day, James and I packed up our tent and drove back to London. At the Chiswick roundabout on the approach into London, an orange-vested peddler was selling copies of the *Standard*. Even from a distance, I could make out the picture of Bowie on the main stage and, in big capital letters on the front page, the three words that made everything all right: "BY TOM SYKES."

Everything had turned out nice again.

## −1,208 DAYS

I got away with the Glastonbury debacle because Clackson basically wrote the story for me. I was his protégé, after all, so he took care of me. But the following year, he retired, and the new guy who took over his desk had none of Clackson's indulgence.

On the very last day of August 2001, I was fired from the *Standard*. The official reason was cutbacks, but coincidentally the ax fell just after I got the name of a friend of the editor wrong in a piece I wrote for the paper. It wasn't just any old friend—it was the actor Richard Harris. I wrote Robert Harris for some reason, and the mistake wasn't noticed until the paper was out on the stands, with a huge story accompanied by full-color pictures on the prized page three spot about how "Robert Harris" was going to be the star of the Harry Potter films. It still makes me cringe.

When I was called into the editor's office, I knew I was about to get whacked. It was like that horrible last day at Eton all over again. It was inevitable that I was going to mess up a crucial detail like this eventually. I was smoking a lot of skunk with James most nights, and my brain rarely defogged during the day.

Sure enough, I was told to go. But because of my staff contract, I was offered a handsome payoff, almost £10,000, to go quietly. Ten grand to quit? I could hardly believe it. Where did I sign?

I couldn't have been happier as I strolled out of the offices of the *Evening Standard* for the last time, declining even to pack up my desk. Drunk on bravado, I wasn't worried in the least about my long-term situation. I would go freelance. I was twenty-seven, and I knew I was a good writer when I focused. I'd just have to stop smoking so much damn pot. I raced up to see James to tell him the news over a few joints.

I didn't actually need much money, I told James as he congratulated me on my payoff and tossed me a big bag of sweet-smelling buds. I had just bought a little house in Golborne Road, just up the street from Notting Hill Gate, with my three sisters, Alice, Lucy, and Plum. We had bought it with money that my granny had given to us in trust when we were children, and the payments on the mortgage we needed on top of the lump sum were just a couple of hundred pounds a month. I could easily cover that with my payoff. For my sisters, who had all moved to New York, it was an investment. For Sasha and me, who got to live there for next to nothing, it was a dream come true.

Sasha and I had been living together for over a year now. We both had the same idea of a good time—going out to the pub and meeting up with mates for a slew of pints. Once I got fired, though, Sasha did start to get a bit annoyed that she had to get up at seven every morning to get to work—she had a job designing the interiors of shops—while I lay in bed sleeping off my hangover.

I was the world's worst freelance journalist. In the first week after I got fired, I wrote a witty piece about the upside of being fired ("The Joy of Sack"). It was the only piece I wrote in three months. I never sold it.

I was sitting at the kitchen table going through the piece yet again on the afternoon of September 11, when the Twin Towers fell in New York. Once I got through to my sisters in New York, I went up to James's and spent every day of the next fortnight there watching the World Trade Center crumble over and over again on TV, smoking grass, and drinking tea before meeting up with Sasha for beers in the evening.

After two weeks, I set about trying to sell my piece, figuring that the papers might be in need of something other than gloom and doom. I couldn't have been more wrong.

"Give it a couple of months, Tom," one short-tempered editor told me. "Nobody really gives a shit about you getting fired right now."

September dragged into October. There was still no work for my stock in trade—light, fluffy articles about nothing—so I didn't bother looking. I spent a lot of time at James's place, and he spent a lot of time at mine.

One night Sasha got home from work to find me, stoned again, lying on the sofa listening to Pink Floyd, munching chocolate, and drinking Diet Coke.

She turned off the stereo and sat down next to me.

"Monkey, I'm really getting scared," she started.

I sat up and tried to concentrate, but my head was swimming.

"Why?" I asked.

"Because you haven't had any work since you got fired," she said. "What are we going to do?"

"It's not like I haven't been trying, Sasha," I snapped defensively. "There isn't any work. No one's commissioning anything."

"Well, maybe if you didn't go and hang out with your other *girl-friend* James and get stoned in his garden all day, you'd be able to find some."

"Look, babe, it's fine; don't worry about it. I've still got all that money from the *Standard*. Don't stress. Things just aren't good at the moment."

"Well, if you're just going to sit around all day, maybe you could at least try and tidy up after yourself then," she said, standing and picking up the empty candy wrappers and drink cans around me. She didn't touch the newspaper, which had rolling papers and clumps of grass and pathetic, torn-up bits of cardboard scattered over it.

The next day, a little shocked by Sasha's outburst because Sasha and I never argued, I rang Toby Young, a friend and journalist who had been fired from almost every newspaper in the UK. He had a look at the "Joy of Sack" piece for me and suggested I send it to a contact of his at GQ magazine.

I duly e-mailed the article and fifteen minutes later got a reply from the features editor, Alex Bilmes. The piece was great, very smart, and funny, he said. He didn't want it, he said. But there was a job open at GQ for an assistant features editor. Was I interested?

Two weeks later, scrubbed, shaved, and with a full forty-eight hours between me and my last joint, I was sitting at a table in the subdued light of the bar in Claridge's Hotel in Mayfair with Alex while the deputy editor, Bill Prince, went to get a round of Bloody Marys. It was five in the afternoon.

Bill was wearing an immaculate, two-piece Savile Row suit from the same tailor as me, Kilgour, which I felt could only be a good omen. The three of us exchanged pleasantries for a few minutes, and then I asked what they were looking for. "Well," said Bill, "we want someone who can manage the front section of the magazine and go out every night as well. We need someone to be our eyes and ears on the ground. If tricorn hats are suddenly hot, we want you to know about it and get it in the magazine first."

Go out every night and look for hats? I could do that, I assured them. I got the job.

Once again, I reflected with some satisfaction as I whizzed home, slightly high from Bloody Marys, I had turned a crappy situation around. Sasha would be delighted. I was getting away with it.

## –1,124 DAYS

I started at *GQ* in the middle of November. My first outburst of public drunkenness came in December, when we had the annual Christmas lunch. I strode into the boardroom at about twelve thirty for my first glass of champagne and ran straight into the guest of honor, a disgraced politician called Neil Hamilton, and his self-described battle-ax of a wife, Christine. Their luck had run low after Neil had been thrown out of the government for corruption, and he and his wife had been reduced to the role of the nation's court jesters, humiliating themselves for money. Their latest stunt had been to pose naked in *GQ*—a revoltingly distasteful sight, as they were both in their fifties, flabby from too many years spent with their snouts in the trough. But the stunt had garnered mountains of attention for the magazine in the British newspapers. And if there was one thing our editor, Dylan Jones, cared about, it was getting attention from the papers.

I was chatting to Neil about his disastrous career when I began to notice that he was literally tipping glass after glass of champagne down his throat. The man was going to be slaughtered. I paced myself by him. For every two glasses he had, I drank just one.

Four glasses for me and eight for him later, we sat down to eat. The lights were dimmed, and we were served smoked salmon, turkey, and Christmas pudding. There was also a lot of wine. About the middle of the lunch, I began to notice that I was feeling very, very drunk. Luckily, I had taken out some insurance against this and scored a wrap of coke off James the night before. I went to the bathroom and did a line, returning to the table reassuringly clearheaded. Another glass of wine? Why not?

At the end of lunch, our managing editor, Claire, started handing out presents. I can't remember what I got. Miles, the art editor, was given a pair of hair clippers.

"Anyone want their hair cut?" he shouted, more in hope than expectation.

Why do I do these things? Why do I do them? I felt my hand going up, and I was shouting, "Yeah, me! Me! Me!"

"Really?" asked Miles.

"Sure," I shouted. "I need a haircut."


## −1,097 DAYS

I woke up the next morning and groaned deeply. Sasha had already gone to work. The alarm clock showed 9:00 a.m. I had to get a move on. What the hell had I done last night? I couldn't remember a thing.

I staggered through to the bathroom to brush my teeth and looked in the mirror.

So *that* was what happened. My head was shaved. Not totally bald, but there couldn't have been more than one-tenth of an inch of hair left.

I ran a bath. A hot bath. The sweating would help me to detox. So I was going to be late today. So what.

I lay in the bath with my eyes closed, and the day before started to come back to me. Miles with his hair clippers. Me sitting on the chair. Everyone standing around, watching, cheering me on.

At least someone had been more embarrassing than I had been. I had a vague memory of Neil Hamilton ripping open his shirt and demanding that one of the girls at the office shave his chest hair. But then again, Neil Hamilton didn't work at *GQ*. He didn't have to go into the office this morning. He wasn't the new boy, who had only been working there a month and should have been trying to make a good impression. Shit, shit, shit.

I was an idiot and a piss head, and now everybody knew it. My haircut would make sure they didn't forget.

Although my hair grew back a little over Christmas, my reputation never really recovered. I tried not to mind. So people thought I was a crazy drunk guy. Well, I was. That was the whole point of being me, right? That was my brand. Although, I reflected, it would have been nice if my editors at my new job had thought that I was smart, intelligent, funny, and witty instead of just plain deranged.

I was on a three-month probation at *GQ*, so when I got back to work in the New Year, I did get serious for a little while. I cut right back on the drinking and smoked almost no dope in the week; and when the three months were up, Dylan called me into his office and told me I was doing well and to keep it up. "You've got opportunities to move up the masthead here," he told me. This was basically a lie, as neither the features editor, Alex, and especially not Dylan or Bill were about to leave. Actually, there wasn't really anywhere to go, but I appreciated the comment and thanked him anyway.

My main job at *GQ* was to edit the front section of the magazine, Details, which covered all the things I liked, such as music, clubs, fashion, nightlife, food, parties, and alcohol. Most nights there were events or parties to go to; as the year wore on, I was out later and later every night. I would go to the event, then head off to a pub to meet my friends Olly, Frank, and usually James.

Often when I got home late at night, Sasha would be asleep; and when she left for work, I would be crashed out. We could go for days at a time just communicating by phone.

On the small Vespa motorbike I had bought to replace my Fiat Panda—I sold the car to James for two ounces of skunk and a gram of coke—I could get from Golborne Road to the Condé Nast offices in Oxford Circus in twelve minutes flat. I had to be there by nine thirty in the morning, and I usually made it by nine forty-five. Alex didn't mind my being late, but Bill had a thing about lateness.

One morning after a particularly heavy night, I didn't get in until eleven. I sat down at my desk and sent Bill an e-mail.

"Sorry I am so late," I wrote. "My bike wouldn't start, and I had to get a bus. Then the bus broke down in Notting Hill, and I had to get a cab."

One second. Two seconds. Three seconds. *Bing!* "Did the cab break down as well?"

I stared intently at my screen, trying fruitlessly to think about what to write back for a few minutes until I couldn't take it anymore. I went outside for a smoke, and Alex followed me. We stood outside the building smoking in silence in the pale English sun. The cigarette tasted stale in my hungover mouth. I felt like shit.

Eventually I spoke. "So I guess Bill copied you on that little exchange," I said.

"Yup," said Alex.

"Am I going to get fired?" I asked.

"No, don't be stupid. Of course you're not going to get fired, Tom," said Alex. Then he gave me the talk. "Bill and Dylan trust me to run the features desk, and I understand that you have to go out every night. But you will get fired if it carries on and you don't pull your weight. I like you, Tom, and you're a great guy, but I can only plead your case so far. Everyone likes you, but you are losing their respect as a journalist. Just sort out the section."

I went back in and sat at my desk, avoiding eye contact with Bill all day. The section was a mess. None of the copy was in. When work ended, I went to the pub. Then I got on the bike and sped up to James's for a joint.

James's house was like a social club for me and my friends. Most of us would pass through at some stage of the evening to pick up a packet of powder or herbs and stay around for a joint and a cup of tea.

## −835 DAYS

The most eagerly anticipated event of the year at *GQ* was the conference. In 2002 we were given the run of a country house hotel in Wiltshire for the annual piss-up. It was a two-day event, but I missed the first night because I was in New York visiting my sisters.

We spent the day doing corporate bonding–type events like clay pigeon shooting and riding three-wheelers through the mud-sodden countryside. But the party in the evening was what it was really all about.

One moment I was having a glass of wine with Peter Stewart, the publisher; the next I was tired and hungry and curling up in bed. I woke up in the morning with a stinking headache, an apple core in my bed, and an uncomfortable feeling that my behavior hadn't been all it might have been the night before.

I got out of bed and looked around for my suitcase. That was when I realized I wasn't in my own room. I was in a girl's room. All my clothes were scattered on the floor. I was naked. Oh, shit.

I was quite alone in the room, so I took a shower and tried to remember what I had done the night before. Despite being a drunken fool, I was proud of the fact I had never cheated on Sasha, and I just had a gut feeling that even though I was clearly in a girl's room, I hadn't done anything really bad.

Oddly, the fact that I was naked in a bed not my own didn't concern me too much as I washed and conditioned my hair in the shower to help get rid of the booze smell. It was part of a pattern. Lately, when I had been really drunk, I had developed a thing about climbing naked into other people's beds. It always amazed me that I did this since, sober, I am a prude. I hate other people seeing me naked. It was one of the main reasons I never went to the gym. All that locker-room stuff gave me the creeps.

But over the past few months, I had climbed into bed first with my friends Hugh and Sarah and then with another couple, Tom and Minnie. Apparently when they asked what I was doing, I would say things like, "But you look so comfy! I just want to cuddle up," and then I would pass out between them.

Still, I figured, as I used the complimentary-size bottle of mouthwash to help freshen my breath in lieu of a toothbrush, it was a shame it had happened at the conference, with work people. I had no idea where my room was, so I dressed in last night's shirt and went down to breakfast.

When I walked into the dining room, thirty faces from the office swiveled toward me and simultaneously laughed at me with friendly contempt. This had been bad, then. I put my arms by my sides to shrug as if to say, *"What, me?"* and smiled knowingly, as if I knew exactly what I had done. No one seemed angry, at least, just highly amused by my antics. I got my coffee and walked over to sit with Alex and Helen, a tall, funny, blonde girl who worked in the art department.

"All right, Sykesy," said Alex as I sat down. "Sleep well?" He rubbed his hands in amusement.

"Yeah," I said as I took a sip of coffee. "Why?"

"Do you remember what you did last night, Tom?" Helen asked me, grinning from ear to ear.

"No, but I suspect I am about to find out." I smiled, trying to be fearless and smooth.

"Well, you were really drunk, and you came into my room," Helen said in her matter-of-fact way. I noticed that all the other staff members were now craning toward our table to listen. Clearly this wasn't the first time this story had been told this morning. "Then you took all your clothes off and climbed into my bed," Helen continued. "So I got out of the bed and tried to get rid of you, but you wouldn't leave. You just kept saying, 'Let me sleep, let me sleep.' Then you picked up one of my tampons and started taking it apart. And I was like, 'Tom, leave now!' but you wouldn't, and you reached out to the fruit bowl and grabbed an apple and started eating it. You were just like, 'I'm hungry!' and that was when I left to go and sleep in Millie's room."

Helen was grinning at me uncontrollably. Everyone listening was laughing at me. I was drenched in shame and embarrassment. I fought to find the magic phrase, the words that could fix everything, make it all okay. But this time, they wouldn't come. The best I could do was to ask, "And you say I was eating an *apple*?"

## −675 DAYS

The bed-crashing incident at the conference became a mini *GQ* legend. For weeks afterward, people would come up to me apropos of nothing and say, in the most shocked and outraged tone they could muster, "An *apple,* you say? Are you *quite sure*?"

The bottom line was that *GQ* stood as much for drunken debauchery as it did for £2,000 suits and cashmere socks. I heard countless times what a great and friendly guy one former editor named Michael VerMeulen was, before I learned that he died of a cocaine overdose at the ripe old age of thirty-eight. In a documentary about Britpop, James Brown, who had been the editor before Dylan, declared that the bathroom was his boardroom and the most important deals when he was editor of *GQ* were struck over lines of weasel dust. He was fired after he oversaw an issue that declared Rommel to be the century's forty-first most stylish man, much to the disgust of Condé Nast's Jewish proprietors, the Newhouse family. He had never checked the issue and had no idea about the inclusion of the mass-murdering Nazi. After he was fired, he came back to the office, saying, "Who put Rommel in?" (It was one of the art editors.)

But the drinking and partying began to impinge more seriously on my capacity to do the job. The front section was a mess. The copy was always late for two reasons: First, the writers who were supposed to be working for me didn't respect me—they were all friends of friends appointed by Bill and Dylan and answered only to them. Second, when the copy came in, I would sigh deeply and bang my already sore head on the desk and then go outside for a cigarette and a coffee rather than start processing it through the system.

As the situation got worse, I became more and more desperate to get to the pub after work (although, unlike one of my predecessors in the same job, at least I wasn't actually going to the pub in the daytime). Alex and Bill would hardly come to the pub with me anymore, and when they did, they didn't get drunk; so I started hanging out with the art department, who loved to drink and drank properly.

My excuses were getting worse. One night I went for dinner at Nobu with Toby Young, who was writing a piece about London Fashion Week for *British Vogue*. After dinner, we went to a nightclub event that was being held for a music business awards show. At the door, they asked who I was, and I declared I was Alex James, the bassist in the band Blur. "This is my . . . entourage." I winked cheekily at the clipboard-wielding hot blonde at the door, putting on a David Bowie voice and pointing to my seven pals.

"Oh, please, come in," she flirted back cheekily to me.

We made it to the bar and ordered vodka and tonics. I reflected on just how calmly I had pretended to be someone else to get us all in. I had done it without really thinking. It just showed how far a little confidence could go. I was actually pretty cool.

## −674 DAYS

Normal drinkers don't really understand how blackouts work. Sure, the first bit is easy to understand—one moment you're questioning whether impersonating trendy bassists is a valid way to get into a party; the next you're waking up in a sweaty bed. You have no memory of what happened in between. The memory chip has been wiped.

But you rack your brains. You were with Toby at Nobu, right, drinking sake. Then the party, where you pretended to be Alex James (very funny). Then I remember the bar . . . nope, nothing. Sasha had already gone to work, so I couldn't ask her. Actually, it seemed kind of late. Where the hell was the clock? Shit, shit, shit. Down to the kitchen. And there's the clock on the stove. Eleven forty-five. *Shit!* You were supposed to be at work two hours ago! Shitting hell!

Okay, the only thing to do was to pretend I was sick. I rang Alex on his cell phone. He answered on the first half ring. "Tom? Where are you?"

"Hey, man, I'm sorry I haven't called. I'm sick. I went for dinner at Nobu last night, and I think I must have eaten a bad bit of sushi."

Silence.

"Alex?"

"Don't move."

Then I heard Alex get up from his desk, clomp his way down the corridor, down the stairs, and into the street. The spark of a lighter. The crackle of burning tobacco. Then Alex was saying to me, "Tom, is this some kind of joke?"

"What? No, man. I just feel really shit. I'm not hungover, I promise, " I said, pacing the kitchen.

"You're not hungover?"

"No, man. Bad sushi."

"Okay, first, Tom, they don't *do* bad sushi at Nobu, and second, you were on the phone to me, ooh, let's see, five hours and fifteen minutes ago!"

Oh, shit. Hot and cold. The clock said 11:47. "What?" I said. I still had no memory.

"For Christ's sake, Tom, you were on the phone to me. I had to leave my cell phone on all night because I was expecting a call from LA. And at four in the morning, you ring. And you're yelling at me, *yelling,* Tom, 'Bilmes, you fucker, get your arse down here now, you wanker.' So I tell you to get lost"—on the other end of the phone, I collapsed onto the sofa and—too late—it all started coming back. We were at that record party doing coke! Shit! Alex wasn't screaming in my ear, like I would have been (and apparently was just a few hours before). He sounded bemused and upset more than angry. "And then you call again at five and again at *six thirty* to *apologize* for calling before." Okay, then he was screaming, "I'm your boss, Tom! I'm your boss. *And you're calling me to tell me how many Es you've done!*"

There was a long silence while all the memories flooded back to me. "Alex, I can't work today. I'm sorry. I really am sorry."

"Sorry doesn't mean anything, Tom, if you just go out and do the same thing over and over and over again." And the line went dead.

## −645 DAYS

It didn't take a psychic to see that sooner or later I was going to get fired from *GQ*. The magazine and I were suffering from mutual contempt. They thought I was useless and were probably right. I was angry with them because they hadn't run a column I had written about getting engaged to Sasha, which had happened at the end of the year. And boy, was I drinking and smoking a lot of weed.

I was sitting at my desk one day when the phone rang. It was Bridget, my sister's roommate in New York.

"Hi, Tommy," she said. "Are you still interested in working out here?"

I had had a twenty-second conversation with her the last time I was in New York about maybe working at the *New York Post,* where she worked. I looked around the *GQ* offices, where everyone hated me and wouldn't even run my engagement column. "Sure," I said.

"Well, the features editor at the *Post*, Faye Penn, is looking for someone like you," Bridget said. *What do you mean, someone like me?* I thought but didn't say. I knew what she meant anyway. Someone young, sharp, and bright. Basically the nondrunk, nonhigh version of me that I was so good at pretending to be when I needed to. "Are you interested?"

Three weeks later, I walked into Dylan's office and announced my resignation. I was going to New York. I've never seen a man look so relieved. The next week, I gave a leaving speech in which I jestingly apologized to Dylan for having conned him into hiring me, and Dylan jestingly gave a speech saying that if it didn't work out in New York, I could always come back to London and "work at *Esquire.*" What a joker!

It was actually a good night. By quitting, I had solved the biggest problem the magazine had faced in the past year, and everyone was relieved that I had jumped before I was pushed.

As for New York, I thought to myself as I danced the night away with Sasha at a nearby bar I had hired for my leaving party, I only knew one thing. I had to cut back on the drink and the drugs, or I wasn't going to last five minutes.

## −605 DAYS

Before I left for America, I wanted to take Sasha to see my dad. She had never met him.

I called Dad up and arranged a meeting at a Mayfair wine bar. It was a warm, early summer evening, and Sasha and I were crazed as we finished packing up the house, which I had sold, making a good profit for me and my sisters. We had ended up with about £40,000 each.

I rode into town on the Vespa with Sasha on the back. Even though this was supposed to be "a quick drink," I had a hunch I was almost certain to drink too much to ride the bike home and would have to leave it locked to a lamppost overnight. It was just impossible not to drink when you were with my dad.

Sasha and I walked into the bar, and there he was, sitting at a wooden table with three of his cronies.

"Aha," my dad said as we walked in, leaping to his feet. "Welcome, welcome."

"Hi, Dad," I said, and gave him a hug, which was what I usually did because it just felt easier to pretend that a hug was normal rather than do what I really felt like, which was shake hands. "How's it going?"

"Not bad, not bad," he said. "Drink?" Then he looked at Sasha. "Drink?"

Sasha was looking confused and tried to smile. Everything always seemed to happen quite fast when my dad was involved. "Er, sure," she was saying.

I stepped in. "Sasha, this is my dad. Dad, this is Sasha, my fiancée."

"What do you want?" Dad was asking her.

"We'll both have a pint of lager, please, Dad," I cut in, trying to take some of the pressure off Sasha.

"Filthy fucking lager!" he exclaimed in disgust. "Well, sit down, and I'll go and get them for you. Are you sure you wouldn't prefer a nice glass of champagne?"

"No, thanks, Dad. A beer will be fine."

He shrugged, made a face of hopelessness, and indicated the three cronies sitting there with him.

"This is Thomas," he said, indicating a very red, portly old gentleman sitting to his right. Then, turning to a skinny, weasel-faced man on his left, "And this is Patrick. Patrick used to be an IRA hitman, so watch what you say or he'll kill you."

"Okay, will do," I said as brightly as possible, then sat down next to him and smiled.

The third guy—a middle-aged, well-fed man in a suit—then said, "Hey? Aren't you going to introduce me?"

"Of course I am," said Dad. "This is Alexander Nikrassov. He's a very prominent Russian, so you have to be reasonably guarded what you say around him as well."

Sasha and I sat down to talk to this unlikely trio while Dad went and got us drinks at the bar. I was a little thrown, as I had been expecting that Sasha and I would meet him on his own. I guess I'd been making the mistake—again—of hoping we could have some kind of sensible conversation. These guys, I reflected, were Dad's insurance against that.

"So, er, how long ago did you get out of the IRA?" I asked the hitman. He gave a mean smile and promptly changed the subject.

Conversation got easier after several pints. Thomas was ranting on about how the European Union was a giant conspiracy and the euro was an evil plot to ruin us all and steal all our money, masterminded by Tony Blair. Nikrassov talked enthusiastically about the financial opportunities afforded by the breakup of the Soviet Union. Dad was doing his usual conversational patter, quoting Shakespeare and Ovid while running through a quick history of modern civilization.

The weird thing about seeing my dad was that although he was undoubtedly there, being charming and funny in his own way, I could never seem to get him to actually engage in the present situation. This time, for example, he didn't ask me anything about the wedding or why we were moving to New York, which, after all, was the reason we had come to see him.

Eventually I tried to prompt him. "So, er, Dad, you know we are moving to New York and getting married, don't you?"

"Yes, yes," he said enthusiastically. "God, I loved New York when I was younger."

Thomas bellowed across the table, "I have never seen such horrendous poverty as I have seen in America, anywhere. Not in the Third World, India, Africa. Never have I seen deprivation like America."

Everybody looked at him uncomfortably for a few seconds and then tried to return to their own conversations.

I remembered my dad going to New York a lot when I was seven or so. His circle of friends ranged from Claus von Bulow to Charlie Schulz. I remembered a story about the time he arrived in New York right after Black Wednesday, the 1987 stockmarket crash, and was hanging out with a Texas billionaire who had been identified that morning as one of the six individuals who had lost over one billion dollars in the crash.

"He was holed up in the top floor of the Carlyle with Bobby

Short playing the piano downstairs," my dad said. "When I asked him what it was like to lose a billion dollars, his only comment was that it might be a good time to try and buy Time/Life. He said the neon clock on their building was a bit bright, and if he bought it, he would be able to turn the clock down a bit."

"Genius," I laughed.

I had a sense my dad was deploying his anecdotes like smoke bombs. In the end, I just gave up hoping that we would get on to something that mattered and surrendered to the party spirit.

"Where did you used to drink when you were in New York?" I asked instead.

"We used to go to El Morocco quite a bit," he reminisced, crossing one leg over the other and holding his champagne glass rather grandly, on a level with his eyeline. It was getting dark outside now, and I was really quite drunk. The bike would have to stay in town overnight.

"El Morocco?" I asked. "What's that?"

But Dad wasn't listening. He was off again. "I remember my friend Jim Jones, who came from Beeville, Texas," he sighed. "He used to call me Chuck because I once leaned into, rather than out of, his Cadillac limo outside of El Morocco and was violently sick into it, rather than, as one more normally would be, onto the pavement."

He laughed at the memory, then added, "Sadly, he was eventually taken away by the men in the white coats."

And so the night went on. Crazy stories and even crazier company. Somewhere along the line, we gave in on the drinks as well and started drinking champagne too. Finally at eleven, the bar closed, and Sasha and I got up to leave.

Dad still had more stories. "Did I tell you about the time I was staying with Claus and had to pretend to be Jewish?"

"No," I laughed.

"I got a crewcut, and it revealed an unknown bald spot on my head. I had to buy a yarmulke on Seventh Avenue to hide it."

Everyone was in hysterics. The Irishman was telling Sasha, "If you get in any trouble in New York, any trouble at all, call us; we can help. We know people in New York, okay?"

"See you later, cock," my dad was saying. "Send us a postcard."

As predicted, we had to abandon the bike and get a cab back home. We finished the packing in a drunken blur.

## −581 DAYS

In most New York stories, the hero arrives in Manhattan with a suitcase and a dream. I pitched up with a suitcase and a hangover.

I had seven leaving parties in London because my US working visa kept being delayed. I finally got it in May. The last party was at terminal three in Heathrow Airport with my friend Olly, whom I had asked to be best man at my wedding in September. As parties go, this one sucked. We sat and drank a couple of pints in a sterile pub in departures until they called my flight.

"Well, I guess this is it," I said as I downed my Guinness.

"About time," said Olly.

"I mean it," I said as I picked up my hand luggage. "I'm really going to cut down on my drinking in New York. And no coke."

"Yeah, right, Tommy," scoffed Olly. Then he caught the fear in my face and softened, asking, "Do you mean it?"

I nodded furiously.

"Good luck, mate," Olly said. "I'll come and see you soon."

We hugged, and I tried to think positive.

Being on airplanes always makes me emotional. I get sloppy and morose as I drink my way through the dislocation of the passing time zones, especially when I am alone. I thought of Sasha. Eighteen months earlier, she had set up her own design business. Now it was beginning to take off. Little did I know that for the next two years, we were going to spend almost half of our time apart, as her business as an artist and designer would continually take her back and forth to Europe.

*Really, I should stop drinking about now,* I thought to myself as we flew over Sasha's house in Ireland and struck out for America, the Atlantic forty thousand feet below us. I imagined the plane blowing up, as I always do on planes, and tried to picture what it would be like to fall that far to your death. It would be okay if I was with Sasha. I would hold her as we went down and tell her I loved her all the way. But falling to my death with the guy in 45B for company? I hit the call button. "Vodka and tonic, please," I asked the stewardess. "Better make it a double."

Seven hours later, I was in a yellow New York cab, bouncing down cobbled streets to my sister Alice's apartment. Alice was two years older than I and had moved to New York about two years earlier, following my sisters Lucy and Plum, who both had high-profile jobs on glossy fashion magazines. Alice was doing well for herself in New York also, and I wasn't too proud to be planning to blatantly hang on to the coattails of my sisters' success.

Alice lived in a giant loft apartment in the supertrendy meatpacking district with two English friends, Bridget—the girl who had introduced me to the features editor at the *Post*—and Claire.

Alice's apartment was above the cheapest supermarket in Manhattan. The only things we felt safe buying there were sealed goods like packets of rice and pasta or beer. Claire used to joke that the place "smelt of coke." It was true that the supermarket definitely had a bizarre odor, and you had to try not to breathe through your nose too much when you were foraging for food or alcohol in there. The checkout line took forever as the derelicts in front of you rifled through their pockets for money-back coupons and argued about the special offers.

But Alice's apartment was amazing. It was one huge, fifteen-hundred-square-foot, wood-floored room that had a kitchen at one end and a TV and sofas at the other, with three box rooms off the side. Alice had said that I could stay there until I found an apartment and Sasha arrived.

My "no coke" rule lasted almost forty-eight hours. I arrived on Thursday night, and by Saturday I was crushing a rock of cocaine under a $20 bill, scraping my credit card over the surface of the note until the drugs were milled into a fine powder. The stuff was half the price it was in England—about $50 a gram—and, well, it just seemed churlish not to take advantage of the market. I chopped out a stubby line with my credit card, inhaled, and time just went *whum!*

At five that morning, I was lying on Alice's sofa, desperately trying to get to sleep. Not a chance. The worry soundtrack was playing on a loop in my head, reminding me that I had to start work at the *New York Post* the next morning, that I was stupid, and that I was going to be in big trouble if I couldn't keep away from the drugs.

Just about then the garbage trucks started. They beeped and crunched their way down Fourteenth Street, five floors down, occasionally pausing to empty huge containers of glass bottles. It sounded like an angry, alcoholic giant was doing his annual recycling trip on the corner of Ninth Avenue.

Unfortunately, the sound of crashing bottles didn't drown out the discussion raging in my head; endless remonstrations and recriminations that remorselessly cataloged how I had screwed up before I even began. I checked my watch. Five thirty. Christ. If I did get to sleep now, I wouldn't be able to sleep the next night. I would show up for work on my first day exhausted.

I heard a door open as Alice's roommate Claire tiptoed to the bathroom.

"Hi, Claire," I said to her as she made her way back.

"Tom," she said, starting, bleary-eyed. "What are you still doing up?"

"I can't sleep," I said, sitting up on the sofa in my sleeping bag. "I feel like a big toxic bag of shit. I am completely screwing this up, and I don't know what to do. I promised myself I wouldn't take drugs out here, and well, here I am, on my second night, off my head on coke. I'm just sitting here worrying about how I am going to sleep tomorrow night, and that's keeping me awake now, and, oh, shit, I don't know. I never should have come." A big tear rolled down my cheek.

Claire sat down on the end of my sofa and patted my knee through the sleeping bag. "You're just anxious," she said. "Really, really anxious. I could give you a Xanax if you want."

"What's Xanax?" I asked.

"It's an antianxiety," Claire said. "It just stops you freaking out about everything so you can get to sleep."

Antianxiety. That sounded good. I was just *anxious*. I looked at Claire. "Please," I said, surprised at the desperation in my voice.

Twenty minutes later, I was gently floating away on a chemical sea of absolution. I pulled the sleeping bag up under my chin, self-consciously pulled a sleepy face for my own amusement, and chuckled to myself. I could still hear the garbage trucks, but now they were only coming through in waves. *Like Pink Floyd,* I giggled, *I am comfortably numb.* Another waterfall of glass reminded me I was in New York. I'd made it. And now I was going to get some sleep.

## −573 DAYS

I woke up early Monday morning on Alice's sofa; showered in her tiny, dilapidated bathroom; shaved; and put on my bespoke Kilgour suit, a freshly pressed pink shirt with silver cuff links, and a woven black silk tie dotted with spots of white. I checked myself in the mirror and clapped my hands, feeling satisfied. If there was one thing I could do, it was scrub up well. People forgive anything in a well-groomed man.

Bridget and I got the subway to work together. She walked incredibly fast down Fourteenth Street to the subway from the apartment, ducking and weaving through the solid sidewalk crowd, glancing over her shoulder to check I was keeping up. It was like trying to follow a flying fish. The street was heaving. I had to turn sideways, suck in my stomach, and flatten my arms by my sides to weave past obese tourists from the Midwest; dart to the left and then right to find a way through the serried ranks of schoolkids walking four or five abreast; and hop down into the road for half a pace or two just to keep Bridget in view.

It was only May, but it was hot that day; and when I got to the subway steps, I was sweating. Bridget had beaten me by a minute and bought us each a bottle of water and a copy of the *Post*. We rattled up to Forty-Seventh Street in about five minutes in an air-conditioned subway carriage. I was used to spending at least forty minutes to go the same distance in London, usually in a hot, sweaty, smelly carriage where your nose invariably ended up in disgustingly close proximity to someone else's armpit. I mentioned my observations to Bridget. She smiled and said, "It's not always like this. Before long, you'll be bitching about the subway just as much as you did about the tube."

I love the first few days at a new job. You just sit around acquiring stationery, checking out the swivel on your chair, and going for an endless round of lunches and coffees. No one expects anything. By Wednesday, when Faye sent me out on my first assignment, I had done little more than send e-mails to my friends back in the UK, put together a few basic story ideas, and work out who was most likely to be at the boozer across the road, Langan's, after work. (The answer, I swiftly discovered, was Steve Dunleavey, the *Post*'s resident drunk.)

My first story was about a very rich, very annoying "Jewish American princess" (JAP for short in New York slang) who had hired a stylist to help her clear out and organize her cavernous walk-in closets. When I got to the apartment, the two of them were having a wild tug-of-war with a Gucci bag, surrounded by empty boxes from Fendi, Dior, and Prada.

"Don't touch the fucking Gucci," the owner, a blonde bitch in her forties who had clearly had a lot of cosmetic surgery, was screaming, pulling the bag.

"You never fucking use it," the stylist, a skinny twentysomething who had black hair in a ponytail and was boiling with ambition (she was the one who had called the *Post* to get coverage for the story), was yelling back, pulling the strap. "Just let it go!"

The battle was eventually settled by an expensive tearing noise. It went on like this all afternoon. After about four hours, I couldn't bear it anymore, and I headed back to the office and wrote it up. The resulting piece ran the next Monday over two pages ("Confessions of a Closet Monster"). My e-mail crashed with all the congratulatory notes and pitches for other stories that rolled in from around the city.

I was on my way. For the first few months, I usually wrote two or three big features a week, always focusing around the general areas of nightlife and going out or fashion and style. Thursday was the day the big "Going Out" section ran, and I more or less ended up making it mine. I was a freelancer, but I was working five days a week, so I was making good money.

But my lifestyle of drinks, dinners, and cocaine was expensive too. Luckily, when I did run short of cash, I had a secret stash in my UK bank account from the proceeds of the house sale. I would sometimes use my British Visa card, which was linked to the account.

Although technically I remained a freelancer, I became the chief nightlife writer for the *New York Post*. Every day, my mailbox was a riot of brightly colored envelopes containing invites to the night's events. Most were thick cards embossed with silver or red type, but if anyone went to the trouble of sending out slabs of Lucite for their party, then you knew it was going to be good. From the second week on, I was out every single night without fail, trying to get under the skin of the city's scene. Because Sasha had not yet arrived, I was still living with my sister and her girlfriends. I hung out and went out with them a lot. I joked that I was an honorary girl.

The very first thing I discovered was that New York has a chronic shortage of eligible single men. Everywhere I went, high-earning, hard-bodied New York chicks would wander up to Alice and engage her in conversation. She would introduce me, and the girls would talk animatedly to me for a little while.

"Oh, right, you are a writer at the *New York Post,* huh? Just moved here, yeah? Oh, you're engaged! Oh, wow, congratulations! When's the wedding . . . oh, will you excuse me? I have to go . . . get a drink."

Being an eligible single guy in New York is like being a kid in a candy store. Being an engaged guy in New York with an absent fiancée is like being a diabetic kid in a candy store. You can look, but try to eat the goodies, and you may seriously damage your health.

## −563 DAYS

The first step in finding an apartment of my own in New York was to abandon all official channels. As I had not been issued a social security number yet by the US government, had no credit record, and was a freelance writer, real estate agents had taken to literally laughing me out of their open houses.

Instead, after three weeks of kipping on Alice's sofa, I logged on to the Web site Craigslist and sublet a walk-up apartment in the East Village. The apartment was so small, you could be in all three rooms at once, and the bath was actually in a cupboard in the kitchen. I had to order an extra-small double bed, which fit into the tiny bedroom with just enough space on either side to jam your hands down to tuck the sheet in. On one side, the windows looked out onto brick walls that were literally twelve inches away.

I didn't really mind the apartment being so small, and I thought the bath in the kitchen thing was kind of bohemian and cool. Best of all, the place was only $1,200 a month—which meant that once Sasha got here, it would be $600 each. It was next door to a tattoo parlor covered in moldings of skulls, but, I reflected, you can't have it all, right?

I missed Sasha a lot. We were due to get married in September, but she was still stuck in Ireland for most of that first summer, trying to finish off the redesign of a hotel bar in Dublin that wasn't working out well and kept delaying her. It rained every single weekend for twelve weeks—big, sweaty, tropical downpours—while at home, they were having one of the finest summers on record.

Without Sasha to go out drinking with, I had lost my partner in crime. We'd speak every day on the phone, and I would tell her which parties I had been to the night before, discuss the intensity of my hangover, and count the days till she was due to arrive in New York.

Still, I wasn't entirely alone. My building, I soon discovered, was swarming with cockroaches, mice, and other unappetizing life forms. When I came back to the apartment late at night and switched the light on, there would be an explosion of insect activity around the sink as dozens of albino earwigs that looked like something out of *Alien* dived for the homely darkness of the drain.

Sasha was able to come over for about two weeks around my twenty-ninth birthday in June. I was so proud of finding the apartment, but Sasha's face fell when she walked in from her cab. It stank of weed—of course, I had found a dealer by this time, who, in true New York style, delivered—and the fridge contained nothing but beer. I showed her the bath in the cupboard in the kitchen, and she did her best to laugh, then said, "Monk, I'm knackered after the flight. I'm going to get an early night."

"What? You're going to bed? Don't you want to go out for a drink?" I asked. "It's your first night in New York."

The panic in my voice panicked me.

"Exactly," said Sasha. "I want to get into bed with my Monk."

"Oh, okay," I said. "Do you want a beer first?" I reached into the fridge to get one for her.

"No, Monk," said Sasha, impatiently now. "I want to get into bed. I'm exhausted from the flight, and I haven't seen you for almost two months."

She walked three paces to the tiny bedroom.

"Okay," I said. "I'll be right through."

I sat on the sofa and finished my beer. Then I rolled up a joint. Then I thought, what the hell, and got another beer from the fridge. It was early. I drank another beer and another until, quite suddenly, it was late and the fridge was empty. But I wasn't tired. Sasha was asleep. I couldn't believe she hadn't wanted to go out. Was this what marriage was going to be like? Boring? She wouldn't notice if I nipped out for a drink.

I tiptoed silently to the door. The wood creaked. Sasha heard.

"Monk?" she said from the bedroom. "Where are you going?"

"I'm just popping out to get something," I said. "I'll be right back."

And I went. I headed straight to Karma on Second Avenue, one of the last bars in New York City where you could legally smoke, and drank whiskey until they closed at four in the morning.

I sat at the bar thinking, *You can't be doing this*; thinking, *Your fiancée's just got back. Are you insane?;* and then thinking, *Well, you may as well have one more shot to help you sleep.*

I kept wanting to leave, but I couldn't . . . or wouldn't.

 *You must go home to your fiancée now. You must go home now; she just got in. Ah, fuck it, give me one more Jack and Coke for the road.*

## −556 DAYS

The next morning, I woke up on the sofa in the sitting room, late and ashamed and horribly hungover. I peeked into the bedroom. Sasha wasn't there. I ran one of my hot baths and smoked a joint while I was in there scalding and sweating myself better. When Sasha finally came back an hour or so later, I was starting to get wrinkly from the water.

"Hi, gorgeous," I said as she came in.

She wouldn't look at me. She was stuffing groceries into the fridge.

"Monkey, I don't think you have to put sugar in the fridge."

She turned to face me, and her eyes were all puffy from crying. I didn't know what to say, so I said the stupidest thing ever. I said, "Are you pissed off with me because of last night?"

"I'm not pissed off; I'm upset," Sasha sobbed back. "I'm giving up a lot to be here, Tom. And we're supposed to be getting married in four months, and you would rather spend the night in a bar than with me when I've just got here?"

"I'm sorry," I said. "I just needed a drink to get to sleep. It won't happen again."

"Well, I don't care," said Sasha. She sat down on the tiny chair at the tiny kitchen table and looked around the tiny apartment and swallowed. She looked at me hard and said, "Maybe there is something wrong if you have to go and drink like that."

"What do you mean? Do you think I should stop?"

There was silence for a few seconds. "I'm not going to nag you about your drinking, Tom," she said. "If you want to drink, go ahead and drink. I'm not going to become some nagging wife."

I was shocked. "But, Monk, if you think I am drinking too much, please tell me."

Sasha sighed. "Tom, of course you're drinking too much if you are going out till five in the morning when you haven't seen me for three weeks and then sleeping on the sofa. I think you should cut down. But I don't see why I should have to be the one who becomes a nag."

"What do you mean?" I asked, genuinely baffled. If she wanted me to stop drinking, all she had to do was say the word.

"Look, Tom," she said, "we both like going out and getting

wasted. That's what a lot of our relationship is based on. We got drunk the first time we met, remember?"

I nodded. Were we really just about getting drunk together?

Sasha carried on, "In Ireland, everybody drinks! All my friends and family drink. So of course I don't want you to stop drinking and become some boring person who never does anything."

"No, of course not," I said, heaving a sigh of relief. Thank God I didn't have to stop drinking after all.

"But the great thing about you, about us, is that we have always been able to hold it together no matter how wasted we get. I like that about you. But last night wasn't funny. It was just . . . weird."

Silence.

"Okay," I said, suddenly ashamed and frightened again, worried she was about to leave me.

I held my nose and submerged my head under the water for a few seconds. What could I say? How could I hold it together?

I burst up into the air again, exhaling.

"I'll cut down," I said. "Really, I will. Everything's going to be fine. You want to go and get some breakfast?"

**−547 DAYS**

My arrival in New York coincided with another notable British import, a swanky private club called Soho House, conveniently located right across the street from Alice's apartment.

Working on the tried and proven premise that people—New Yorkers especially—always want what they can't get, Soho House had become insanely popular because the club would let hardly anyone join. It had less than a thousand members in the first few months, all of whom had to pay an annual subscription of $1,000. A disproportionately large number of those thousand individuals had been invited to join by my absurdly social brother-in-law Euan, who was on the membership committee for the club.

Euan was married to Lucy, Plum's twin sister; and although I was not a member of Soho House (I couldn't spare the thousand bucks), I could usually get past the dopey door staff at ground level by dropping Euan's name at the door. Then I would go through to the back of the lobby, step into the leather-padded elevators, and be whisked up to the sixth floor of the building, which was decorated in rich, masculine leather and wood. The seating area was dominated by huge armchairs and sofas with supermodels and actresses artfully sprawled over them.

If Euan wasn't there, which was unlikely in the first few months of the club's existence, one of my sisters or one of my British friends was likely to be; and I would just discreetly look at the logbook on the front desk, where members had to sign in, and say their names instead. It all meant that Soho House quickly became my default hangout spot in the first few months.

The bar at Soho House was expensive, but not much more so than any other trendy bar in New York. A cocktail was about $12, a bottle of champagne less than a hundred. The expense was easily justified by the parade of stars that flowed in. Ethan Hawke, Uma Thurman, and Gwen Stefani would all hang out there in a startlingly low-key way. I always got more excited by the British celebs who would show up: David Bowie; Eddie Izzard; and on one memorable occasion, David Beckham and his wife, Posh Spice, who were attending a party thrown by *Vogue* editor Anna Wintour.

So everything was going according to plan in August 2003. I had been in New York for about three months, and I was writing the "Going Out" pages every Thursday. It was a great job for discovering the city. I wrote about the best cocktails in town, which of the new, hot restaurants and hotels had the best bar scene, and which clubs were best for rubbing shoulders with models and celebrities. The only thing I was forbidden to write about was Soho House, which had a strict "no press" rule. I started to get messages from restaurant publicists inviting me to check out the new venues they were promoting, promising they would "take care" of the check.

I told Euan about these solicitations. "Nice one," he said. "TFR."

"TFR?" I asked quizzically.

"Yeah, baby," said Euan. "Total free ride!"

## −520 DAYS

The only problem was that I had been on a monstrous bender ever since I arrived. All my good intentions to cut down on alcohol and drugs had come to nothing. It was a case of New York, same old me.

Or possibly even worse me. In London, a shot of alcohol is a carefully measured 25 milliliters. In New York, they keep pouring vodka into your glass until you say to stop. In London, the bars close at eleven. In New York, even the average neighborhood pub was open till four in the morning. And in London, I had to pay for my drinks. In New York, thanks to my job writing nightlife features for the *Post,* people couldn't give me enough free booze.

The killer, though, was that despite having promised Olly I would stay away from drugs, I was doing more cocaine than ever. Coke was cheap and pure compared to what I had been used to in London, and the drug seemed to go well with New York's frenetic pace. And everyone else was doing it. It was normal, and so was I.

A few familiar problems were starting to recur. I kept getting to work later and later in the mornings because I would oversleep. I always seemed to be broke, waking up with a pocket full of crumpled receipts and a few single dollar bills, despite the fact I was earning good money at the *Post.* I withdrew cash from my English bank account, the house sale money, more and more regularly. It was soon down to about £25,000. I would feel a rush of guilt and panic in my head whenever I thought about how I was frittering away my inheritance, but I told myself that there had been a lot of expenses involved in setting up our new life in New York.

The latest of these was moving out of the East Village. Sasha had found a much more spacious one-bedroom apartment on Fifty-Fifth Street in midtown Manhattan. It was a splendid, cockroach-free place, with plenty of natural light and wood floors. It was reasonably cheap because it was a fourth-floor walk-up, and it was in midtown. I came to love everything about our block, from the Robert Indiana LOVE statue on the corner of Fifty-Fifth and Sixth, to the pub where they would let you smoke after midnight, to the amazing

French restaurant opposite us called La Bonne Soupe, where we had swiftly befriended the owner, Yves, and the manager, Jean. Whenever Sasha was away taking care of her business back in Ireland or London, I lived almost exclusively on their famed onion soup.

But the drinking was crazy. After I slept in till two and missed an eleven o'clock appointment with a men's clothing designer who was going to let me strut the catwalk in his show during fashion week for a story, I decided to try to quit drinking for a week to prove I wasn't an alcoholic. I got good and drunk on Sunday night and ordered $100 worth of pot. Then every night for the rest of the week, I smoked huge quantities of weed before going to the cinema. I managed to get to Friday night without drinking.

That Friday, I went to join Euan and a few other friends for dinner at Soho House. We sat down to eat, and I decided that since I hadn't had a drink *all week* (well, since Sunday, anyway), just one glass of wine with dinner couldn't hurt. The waitress came over to take our order. The other guys at the table ordered a bottle of wine, and when the waitress turned to me, I ordered a steak and asked, "Also, I would like a glass of Merlot. But could you please bring it to me with my main course?" She nodded, went away, and returned immediately with my wine, which she placed on the table in front of me, then scooted back to the kitchen before I could protest.

I was furious. Now I had to sit here through the appetizers with this glass of wine in front of me and not drink it if I wanted to have a glass of wine with my steak. I waved at the waitress, who came hurrying over.

"Hi. How can I help?" she asked.

"Yeah, the thing is, I ordered this glass of wine to come with my main course," I said. "But they brought it right away. Could you take it away and bring it with my main course, please?"

The waitress looked at me peevishly and gave her eyes a quarter roll. It was a busy Friday night. "Why don't you just keep that glass of wine and drink it when your main course comes?" she suggested patronizingly.

"Because," I snapped, "I only want to drink one glass of wine, and if you leave this here, I'll drink it now."

I realized too late what I had said and how I had said it. The air at the table changed. The temperature dropped a couple of degrees, and then it got very warm. My brother-in-law and his friends stopped talking and looked at me. So did the waitress. She picked up the glass of wine and marched off with it to the kitchen, shouting, "Cancel the glass of wine," at the top of her voice. *Bitch,* I thought to myself.

Eventually it was time for the main course. The waitress came over with our plates. I tried to be ingratiating. "Could I please have that glass of wine back?" I asked.

She looked at me in utter disbelief. "You want a glass of wine now?"

"Yes, please," I said. "That's what I said in the beginning. I asked for a glass of wine with my main course."

"Are you sure about that?"

*Bitch.*

The waitress brought the wine back to our table.

"Thank you," I said, dismissing her, my voice saying, "This is *her* fault."

I drank the wine as slowly as I could with my steak. It tasted so good. The week of abstinence—admittedly foreshortened—had been worth it. I could taste the wine's hundreds of different flavors exploding around my tongue. The slight smokiness. The tannic bite. The *alcohol.*

God, it was good. It was so good, in fact, that I went up to the roof deck immediately afterward and drank six Margaritas to celebrate the success of my little experiment.

## −489 DAYS

I organized a massive TFR when Euan and my sister Lucy had their baby boy, Heathcliff. Lucy didn't want to come out, and Sasha was still in Ireland preparing for our wedding, so I made it an all-boy affair. I rang up one of my best restaurant-owning friends, Jean-Luc, who had a sleek bistro on the Upper West Side, and asked if he would throw a dinner for us.

"Tommy Sykes!" he said when I identified myself. "Of course you can come here for dinner! How many are you?"

"About twelve," I said.

I'm told it was a night to remember. We started off at JL, where we worked our way through cocktails, wine, and dinner. We left a tip for the staff, but the bill—which must have topped $1,000—was taken care of by Jean-Luc. Next stop was the Penthouse Executive Club, a strip joint on the West Side, where I had called ahead to get us all free entry. It was depressing and sleazy in the way that strip clubs always are. The idea always sounds great—the reality of some desperate East European girl shaking her ass in your face tends to be somewhat less thrilling. We didn't hang around long. We wanted to get to Soho House. The club was the very apex of cool.

This is how I remember it: I was standing by the bar ordering drinks at first. I was drinking big New York buckets of martini, feeling very drunk. Then we were standing in a circle in the middle of the room. It was very late, and we were the only people left there. One of our group—in fact, a fairly senior guy in the publishing world—pulled out a joint and lit it.

Most of my memories of things that happen to me when I am in a drink or drug blackout are just fragments. This time, I can remember seeing my leather shoes outlined on the tessellated wooden floor of the bar, two olives parked one above the other in the empty glass on the bar, and my friend pulling out the joint. Then I saw the flare of the lighter as he lit it, him smiling and laughing, and me holding the joint between my thumb and first two fingers, taking a deep draw.

In retrospect, it's easy to say that lighting up a joint anywhere in public was clearly not a smart move. The smoking of *cigarettes* had been banned in New York just three months before, so there wasn't even any tobacco smoke to cover the smell of the weed. The next thing I remember, a lot of people were shouting, and I was saying, "All right, all right! Just don't touch me, okay? Don't fucking touch me!"

I refused to leave the bar. It was past two in the morning, but I wouldn't be moved. I demanded they go and get the manager, Podge, out of bed from his apartment three blocks away to throw me out in person.

### −488 DAYS

I woke up late for work the next morning and called Euan on my way down Sixth Avenue to the offices of the *Post*.

"Hey, man, great night last night," I said when he answered.

Silence. Then, "Do you remember what you did last night, Tom?" he asked me.

"Er, yeah. We went to JL, then that strip club, then Soho House...."

I took a sip of Gatorade. Something had happened. I sighed and gave up. "No, I can't remember, man. What *did* I do last night?"

He told me.

"Oh, shit," I said.

I called Podge to apologize, but I was banned from the club. Euan put in a special word for me, and the owner of the club, Nick Jones, agreed to ban me for three months, after which time I would be allowed back in as long as I had a family member to vouch for me. It reminded me of the time I was rusticated at school. Over the next three years, I was banned from Soho House a record three times.

Just before I was due to get married, in September 2003, the gossip pages of the *New York Observer* got hold of the original story. I was terrified that if they ran an item about how I had been smoking pot in public, the *Post* would fire me. What a wedding present that would be.

It reminded me of what my friend and fellow party animal Godfrey Deeney had told me a few months before, when we were drinking late one night. "You're a good lad, Tom, and New York loves you at the moment," he said. "But if you screw up, and you get caught screwing up, they'll drop you so fucking fast you won't even see the sidewalk before you hit it."

I was about to be dropped. I could see the pavement rising to meet me.

I decided my best hope for the *New York Observer* was to obfuscate. I admitted to the reporter who eventually called me that I had been banned for smoking—but I denied it was pot. I tried to make a self-effacing joke about how the Brits were bad tippers and hoped they would run that instead.

I ran out of the house to pick up the paper the following Monday.

At **Soho House**, the Brit-packed private club in the meatpacking district, the **Sykes** name is something of a mainstay. *Marie*

*Claire* editor at large **Lucy Sykes** is a member, as are her sisters **Plum** and **Alice**. But it looks like brother **Tom** has been banned. According to **Soho House** committee member Tim Geary, Mr. **Sykes** has been banned "because he's not a member" but frequently attempted to gain entrance to the club as if he were.

Though Mr. **Sykes** confirmed that he is not a member of the club, he disputed some of the finer points of Mr. Geary's statement. Mr. **Sykes** said he was banned for three months in the summer, but has since been allowed to cross the threshold once more as a guest of his family members. "I was basically asked to stay away for a couple of months during the summer because I was smoking"—Mayor Bloomberg's smoking ban extends to private clubs—"and being obstreperous, and in true Brit fashion, I think, I wasn't tipping enough, but I've only got my Britishness to blame," Mr. **Sykes** said. "I completely understand and I put my hands up to it."

I laughed and laughed and laughed. I was standing on the corner of Fifty-Fifth and Sixth, and I had to sit down on the black metal base of the LOVE statue because I was laughing so hard. I laughed harder than the crack addicts who used to congregate there late at night did when they had been smoking their stuff.

Everything was working out fine. A few days later, Sasha and I flew to Ireland, where we were married.

## −495 DAYS

I used to hate Wednesdays because at my primary school, they made us do country dancing on a Wednesday. We had to line up and prance around the sports hall to the tune of the Flying Scotsman. At Eton, Wednesday was the day when we were supposed to do "cadet corps"—basically pretend to be in the army and develop the skills and mind-set necessary for a career killing poor people in hot places.

All that changed when I got to New York, though. Now I hated Tuesdays. Every Tuesday, there was a features meeting on the tenth-floor offices of the *Post* at 10:00 a.m. It was the earliest I ever got to the office. Usually I wouldn't show till midday. Well, I was the night-life writer, so surely it was only natural that I should be a late-to-bed, late-to-rise kind of guy, right? Being late was part of my *job*.

But Tuesday was the one day a week when I couldn't be late. The meetings always filled me with dread. The features editor, Faye, sat at the end of a long table in one of the conference rooms, and the reporters sat around the edge. It looked like a dinner party, but if you didn't have any ideas, it felt just like a firing squad.

On Monday nights, I would be gripped with fear and start scribbling down ideas in my notebook. The long lists paid testament to my toxic lifestyle and melted brain. "Sake—is it hot?"; "Caipirinhia—the new Mojito?"; and "Hangover cures—a road test."

Whenever I was really stuck, I'd propose a classic stunt, where I would get dressed up, get photographed doing something outrageous, and then write eight hundred funny words about it. I loved doing stunts. In the UK, I had been known for them ever since the tights photo gave me my first brush with notoriety. I had dyed my hair blond ("Do blonds really have more fun? Our man with the peroxide finds out!") and ridden a horse named Diesel around London to "beat the fuel strike" when militant lorry drivers blockaded the country's petrol refineries to protest high British fuel prices. I was always a little jealous of my friend Tom Newton-Dunne, who worked at the British tabloid the *Mirror* and did the ultimate stunt when he was photographed playing pool in the nude with a crazy guy who kept getting arrested for attempting to walk the length of Britain naked. He's now the defense correspondent at the *Mirror*—Tom, that is, not the naked hill walker.

In New York, I started out small. I smuggled a dog into the cinema in Times Square ("Pup quiz—Where can you really take a dog in NYC?"), then devoted several nights to lighting up cigarettes in bars in an effort to demonstrate that the smoking ban was being widely flouted ("This way to the smoke-easy!").

Stunts were embarrassing, but readers loved them. And I was never in any doubt about the strength of my egotism. I adored seeing my face plastered all over the front page of the features section. It was always a thrill—even if I was wearing lingerie. My e-mail would ping reassuringly all day with congratulatory messages from publicists and not-so-good-natured insults from my friends for stripping myself of any remaining dignity in pursuit of a byline.

What I really wanted, though, was a regular column. A column that fit around my heavy-drinking, hard-partying lifestyle, which I could get paid to write every week. So one Tuesday morning, I suggested we needed a new bar column.

"What's the idea?" asked Faye.

"Well, I figure there's two ways of looking at the New York scene," I said. "Either you can do a massive bird's-eye view of the whole thing—you know, '100 reasons why New York is still the best city in the world'—or you go totally, totally micro and put a tiny area under the microscope. Like, 'What's happening on the corner of Twelfth Street and Third Avenue?' "

Faye looked interested for a moment. She was a tough editor; and if she didn't like your idea, she let you know fast, usually using the word *sucks*.

"I like the neighborhood idea," she said to me, then asked her deputy, "Didn't we have a plan for something like this once? Wasn't it called Block Party?"

"That's a *great* name," I said, pressing, my heart beating harder than the barman at the Passerby Bar—a favorite spot on Fifteenth Street with a flashing floor straight out of *Saturday Night Fever*— shook my martinis.

"Let's call it Block Party," I continued, on a roll now. "Each week, I can write about all the bars and the nightlife character of a different block. People want local right now."

Faye hesitated for a fiftieth of a second. *She's going to call me on it*, I thought. *She knows it's just an excuse to get wasted on their dime.*

Instead I heard her say, "Okay, let's do it." Then she switched her attention to someone else in the room. "Farrah, what you got?"

Farrah started talking about her ideas, but it was all white noise. A little man in my head was shaking a bottle of champagne and popping the cork. There was an explosion of bubbles and cheers.

I called Sasha to tell her the news the moment I got out of the meeting.

"Where will we start?" she asked.

"I don't know. Anywhere. There must be a million bars in New York. A thousand blocks to choose from. This one will run and run."

Over the next year, I wrote about fifty Block Party columns. If I thought I had the greatest job in the world before, now I really did. *I was the bar columnist for the* New York Post.

My drinking problem was no longer a liability. It was a qualification, a vocation, a career. All my life had been leading up to this.

I was paid $300 for each column, but that wasn't the lure of Block Party. Sure, $300 a week helped pay the rent, but much more important, as the column began to get a following, I was besieged by restaurant publicists inviting me to go and eat for free at their fancy establishments and put them in the column.

Thus began in earnest the year of freebie living. I would get to the office by midday and sit at my piled-high, chaotic desk, listening to my voice mail and deleting everything in my e-mail that wasn't a potentially interesting drinking opportunity. The publicists obviously couldn't say anything as blatant as, "We'll give you a free five-course dinner and all the wine you and your wife can drink if you write about us." They used code words instead. They would say, "Let me know when we can set that up for you," "We'll take care of you," or my personal favorite, "Just take care of the staff," which meant, "Please leave a healthy tip."

Sasha and I lived a bizarre double life. We would have to scratch around behind the sofa to find enough quarters to get eggs for breakfast, but by nine that night, we would be eating a $50 egg as a starter at dinner. I'm thinking of one egg in particular here, at the uptown restaurant davidburke&donatella. The egg had been painstakingly hollowed out, the top cut off in a perfect humpty-dumpty crown. The shell was filled with a delicious onion flan mixture, which had been poured back into the egg, baked, and lovingly topped with caviar.

After work, I would either go to the pub or head home to change, and then Sasha and I would take the subway to the stop nearest the restaurant to save on cab fares. We would announce ourselves to the host at the Biltmore Room, the Strip House, or Lever House, and the show would begin.

First up was usually the general manager, who would show us to our table while I asked some well-practiced questions to cement my status as a VIP journalist to whom it would be in their interests to give special treatment. How long had they been open? ("About a month, now, and we have been packed every night.") What was the culinary focus of the kitchen? ("Italian, sir. The chef is famous for the calf cheek fettucine.") Oh, and did they have an extensive wine list? ("We have over two thousand bottles, sir, with a focus on the great vintages of the Languedoc region.")

Once we were seated at our table, gleaming with more glassware and cutlery than we used at home in a week, the just-French-enough headwaiter or maître d' would appear. He would talk us through the menu and then tell us he would give us a few minutes to think about our order. In the meantime, would we like a cocktail or some wine?

At this moment, Sasha and I would look at each other and raise our eyebrows as if to say, "Well, shall we? I mean, we don't usually, but *shall* we, just this once?"

The cocktails would arrive, and the waiter would ask if we knew what we would like to eat.

"No," I would reply, setting aside the menu with an air of defeat. "We'd like to ask a favor. Could you please just choose for us? This menu looks so fabulous, and we don't want to miss anything. We want to try whatever the chef thinks is the very best on the menu."

The waiter would smile, flattered. "Certainly, sir. And for the wine?"

"Is there a sommelier?" I would inquire. "This wine list looks so fabulous, and we really don't want to miss anything there, either. . . ."

Once the waiter had left our table, Sasha and I would grin at each other in dizzy disbelief. Was this really happening?

## −203 DAYS

Week after week—sometimes several times a week, in fact—I inhaled deeply at the intoxicating trough of New York restaurant publicity. Five-course dinners with three bottles of wine, preceded by cocktails and suffixed by brandies, became the norm. I became bolder, ordering $100, $150 bottles of wine. On one occasion, I asked the sommelier to bring me the best Italian wine he had, and he actually did it. I began to say I needed a table for four or *six* people, and Sasha and I would bring friends or my sisters and their husbands or boyfriends. It was absolutely outrageous.

The tips alone became a major financial burden. For a $1,000 dinner, you really have to tip $250 in New York. If it was $250 I didn't have, so what. I would put it on my credit card—linked to my rapidly depleting house sale money—and forget about it.

Sasha loved going out and drinking as much as I did. The difference was that I was *never* ready to go home after dinner. Sometimes Sasha would say she had had enough. Couldn't we call it a night?

I would get into a mood. *Doesn't she understand?* I'd think, as I called to the waiter for a grappa to wash down dessert. I couldn't write a column about just one restaurant. I had to check out the other bars on the block. It was my *job*. The column was called *Block Party*, not, well, *Expensive Restaurant*—although that wasn't a bad idea, actually.

Usually, I won the argument. So on we would go, into the night, into the party, me leading the way, Sasha following, sometimes reluctantly, sometimes not, maybe with a few other friends we had taken for dinner bringing up the rear, a merry little band of drunks. Into every bar on the block we would go. "We'll just check out their martinis," I would say. "Research," I'd wink and chuckle manically.

One of my favorite areas in the city was the strip of hip bars starting at the corner of First and First, and one week I decided to cover the block for the column. We started off with dinner and cocktails at a Moroccan place called Chez es Saada. It was about ten by the time we finished dinner, and I wanted a cigarette. The fact that smoking had been banned didn't stop me from lighting one up. I hid the cigarette under the table. Sasha looked at me disapprovingly. "Tommy," she said, "don't smoke in here. It's really rude. They've just given us an amazing dinner."

"They don't mind," I said, and I called over a waiter and ordered another cocktail—a Steve McQueen ("Makers Mark, blackberry nectar, and fresh lemon juice)—to make the point. The waiter said nothing about the smoke rising from under the table. He knew I was from the *Post,* I thought. He wouldn't *dare.*

By eleven, we were ready for the next stop on our journey. There were two bars almost next to each other on the block, Starfoods and Elephant, and we spent the rest of the night bouncing between the two of them.

Our English friend Anna-Louise was in Starfoods with a bunch of her mates, so we spent most of the rest of the night there. I let the manager know, through Anna, who I was, and the drinks flowed freely.

The last thing I remember was being on the dance floor with Anna, and she was shouting something into my ear. Some guy was a bastard.

"Who?"

"The manager at Elephant," she said. "He's a bastard. I was seeing him. He said he would pick me up in his car the other day and left me on the LIE for three hours."

"What?" I said. "Why?"

"Because he's a bastard. Can you put the fact that he's a bastard in your column?"

I laughed. "Er, I dunno, Anna."

"Oh, please, please, please," she said. "Please!"

She really was a lovely girl. "Well, okay, I'll try," I said.

## −202 DAYS

*Daylight. Where am I? No Sasha. She must have gone out already. Why am I still wearing all my clothes from last night? Why am I on the sofa, not in my bed?*

I notice a half-burnt joint that must have been unraveling all night, spilling burnt marijuana and tobacco all over my white shirt. I must have tried to smoke it last night. It's almost eighty percent weed. That's lucky, I think, guessing that's why it went out rather than burning down the house—or a hole in my leg.

My head throbs violently. My mouth tastes of alcohol—stale whiskey and sambuca.

What did I do last night?

I dig into my pockets. They are stuffed full of mashed-up receipts with crazy signatures and single dollar bills, but there is also a small notebook in there. I pull it out and look at it with interest.

It's my notes for the evening. They say, "Chez es Saada, Moroccan. Steve McQueen. Elephant, Thai—cool. Starfoods—hipster crowd. Dancing. Manager of Elephant bastard says Anna. Mars Bar. Home 4:00 a.m."

I look at the notebook like an archaeologist examining evidence of an ancient civilization. Believe it or not, this actually qualifies as pretty detailed notes for Block Party. It's lucky I have them, because I can't remember a thing. I look at the scribble again. I actually went to the Mars Bar after all that? The Mars Bar, on the corner of First and Second, is a major, major dive, with broken chairs, layers of solid graffiti on the wall, and filthy toilets. It's one of my favorite spots.

I start unfolding the receipts on my bed, counting the bills that remain. Somehow I spent over $200 over the course of last night. I feel sick at the realization. It doesn't make any sense. Dinner was free, after all, and so were the drinks in Starfoods. How the hell did I get through $200? I look in my wallet again just to check, and I see an empty cocaine bag.

Oh, yeah, I remember now. Someone ordered some coke, and I ended up paying for it. Fifty dollars or whatever. I groan and lie back on my bed. I check the clock. Eleven thirty-four. Not too bad, I suppose. I can make it in by twelve thirty. I suffer for my art.

## FIRST THINGS FIRST

### Block Party by Tom Sykes

*The easiest thing about getting to this part of town is the cab ride there—all you have to say is First and First. The hardest thing is leaving: Block Party didn't make it home until 4 am—and that was a school night.*

*Kick off at the Moroccan-themed basement of Chez Es Saada with dinner and a "Steve McQueen" cocktail and admire the elegant crowd, then head for Elephant, a Thai joint with a great bar and an infectious beat. Don't get too cozy with the staff though. Sources told Block Party the manager's a heart-breaker. (He didn't return calls by press time.)*

The editor responsible for overseeing the column sent me an e-mail the next day. "Love the column on First and First. It's great."

I leaned back in my chair and cracked my fingers. Today's hangover was subsiding. I loved this town. I could not believe how great my job was. I loved Block Party. At last, I had done it. I really was getting paid to go out and get wasted.

My head hurt most mornings, and my checking account was a disaster zone, but I was living an incredible life. Free dinners, drinking in every bar around town—and now publicists were even sending bottles of liquor to my office in an effort to get me to write about them. I was the party, bar, and nightlife correspondent for the *New York Post*. Result.

There were a few niggling issues, though, which I preferred not to think about. I was drunk every night. Sasha had decided that the problem was drinking whiskey, which she claimed brought on "the whiskey madness," so I had been banned from drinking that anymore. My heart hurt and palpitated with alarming frequency from all the coke I was doing and weed I was smoking. I hadn't had sex for days—weeks?—because I was always too wasted at night, and Sasha would be gone in the morning. I felt ashamed every time I got money out of my house account, which now had less than £10,000; but I couldn't expense the blow or the $100 restaurant tips, could I? I was too clever to put in $200 worth of receipts for Block Party. Forty dollars, maybe—you know, a drink in every bar. That's what a normal person would have. Not six drinks in every bar. I didn't want to give the game away. The bar owners knew I was into getting wasted and high, but I didn't want to give my editors at the *Post* reason to suspect it. I didn't want to blow my cover. Not now, when everything was going so well. I didn't want to think about all that shit. I wanted to think about tonight. I wanted to go out.

I called a publicist.

"Hi, it's me."

"Hi, Tom. What can we do for you?"

"Can you set me up for dinner for four tonight, please?"

I hung up and flipped through my Rolodex, wondering which of my pals would be game for a spot of "research" tonight.

## −150 DAYS

In July 2004, midway through my second year at the *Post,* Ian Spiegelman, one of the regular contributors to the *Post*'s gossip column, Page Six, was sacked. One drunken night, he had fired off an e-mail to a double-crossing source, Doug Dechert, in which he threatened, among other things, to "push [his] face inside out in private or public" and referred to him as an "aging trust-fund pussy." Proving that drunken typing can be every bit as dangerous as drunken driving, Dechert immediately forwarded the e-mail to our rivals at the *New York Daily News,* and Spiegelman was toast by breakfast.

Covering for staff vacations, I had worked a few shifts on Page Six, so when Ian was fired, I was given a regular shift on the column every Friday. Page Six runs every day of the week in the *Post* (although, through an accident of history, the column is never actually found on page six of the newspaper), and it is undoubtedly the most powerful bit of print real estate in the city. Everyone in New York reads Page Six every day, so anyone who has anything to promote is desperate to get a mention in the column. There were items every day about who had been seen doing what to whom the night before, and every club or bar owner wanted to make sure it was their establishment's name that got attached to the boldfaced names we mentioned.

Page Six was really three people. There was the editor—the

unflappable, deadpan Richard Johnson—and his two deputies, the feisty, fast-talking, and foulmouthed Paula Froelich and the whip-smart and charming professional night owl Chris Wilson. Being the bar columnist for the *New York Post* had given me the keys to the city, but being the bar columnist who also had a regular gig on Page Six was like getting a special bunch personalized with my name spelled out in diamonds and gold.

It also gave me another partner in crime. Chris had become my best friend since I had been in New York. First and foremost, this was because Chris was always up for going out and drinking until the early hours of the morning. I only had to get up for work one day a week (Fridays had taken the place of Tuesdays as my new least favorite day), but Chris had to be in the office every day at ten thirty, Monday through Friday. Ten thirty doesn't sound very early, but when you're out till four in the morning, it's plenty early enough. Chris was late for work more often than not, but he would often stay on in the evening after Paula had left and help put the page to bed, so it all seemed to balance out. And a column like Page Six had to have someone out there walking the walk of the world that the page talked about.

Chris was the single greatest person to go out partying with in New York City. He knew all the nightlife characters; and no matter which club or bar we pitched up outside, the bouncers and bar staff would welcome Chris (and me and anyone else who happened to be with him) with open arms. Chris was outrageous, hilarious, and charming, and he never gave a damn what anyone thought or said about him. And unlike Sasha, Chris was always up for going out as hard and as late as, if not later than, I was.

Chris and I were a team. He believed, as I did, that getting drunk and partying all night made you a more effective chronicler of the nightlife scene. He understood that drinking was an essential part of the job. One day we'd change—just not right now.

"You couldn't do this job if you were sober," Chris told me one morning as we sat in his apartment polishing off the night with a six-pack of beer and listening to Black Flag. "There is so much at your disposal as a reporter on Page Six," he said. "I mean, think about it. There are two or three events every night, private parties where you not only have a full entrée, but you get your ass totally kissed. You never wait in line; you never pay for a drink. You don't have to deal with all that bullshit around the clubs. We have super-human nightlife powers."

I spent more and more time hanging out with Chris. We ran into Bridget one day when we were leaving work to go to the pub across the street, Langan's, and she said, "Oh, my God; it's the terrible twins."

"The terrible twins"—I liked that.

Chris was one of the few people I had ever met who drank his beer at the same speed as I did. Usually when I was with a group of people and I finished my beer and said, "Right, who wants another?" everyone would say, "I'm okay" or "I'm still working on this one." But with Chris, when we got to Langan's, it was like, "Beer?"

"Yup."

"Beer?"

Chug-a-lug-lug.

"Sure, why not?"

Work was on Forty-Seventh Street, and Chris lived on Forty-Ninth. After a few drinks at the pub, we would sometimes head back to his place for a joint to keep the ball rolling.

If there was one area where Chris disappointed me, it was his appetite for weed. I could (and frequently did) smoke weed all day and all night, but after a puff or two, Chris would hand the joint back to me and decline to smoke anymore. "I'm gonna be wiped out," he'd say. "How can you smoke so much of that stuff?"

I didn't really know the answer. I would buy ounce bags of

marijuana for about $100 and just smoke and smoke and smoke until it was gone. Usually, after the first or second joint, I would start to feel weak, tongue-tied, or paranoid, but that never stopped me. I would think that another one might make me feel better. I was like one of those people who can't stop washing their hands, except I couldn't stop smoking pot. More times than I can remember, I would flush all my marijuana down the toilet, only to find myself frantically calling my dealer a few hours later to arrange another delivery. I would catch myself for a moment and think, *This is insane*, but it made no difference. I just wanted to have one more hit.

Although Sasha never chastised me about my drinking—she liked to drink almost as much as I did, after all—she hated me smoking weed. I took to sneaking joints out of the bathroom window to try to hide my habit.

Every night was different but the same, with a revolving cast of characters. Sometimes I would call Sasha, and she would meet us at the pub for a few drinks. Sometimes we would head out for a lavish dinner at a newly opened restaurant, running up a check for several hundred dollars in the full confidence we would never see a bill.

More often than not, dinner was a launching point for the rest of the night. At some point, someone—sometimes me—would say, "Want to get some blow?" I would hand over $50 to a guy who had materialized out of the night and twenty minutes later be chopping out rails of coke in the bathroom. That was when you knew this was going to be a late one. That was also when I knew what our ultimate destination that night would be: Siberia.

It was through Chris that I met Tracey Westmoreland, the fearsome-looking, bewhiskered ex-bouncer who owned Siberia, the notorious dive bar on Fortieth Street between Eighth and Ninth avenues.

Siberia was a crucial part of any New York night out with Chris. Sure, we would be made welcome at all the fancy bars and clubs around town—Marquee, Bungalow 8, Hiro—and even served a check-free bottle of vodka. But come three in the morning, all the glitz and the glamour could never rival the filthy lure of Siberia.

You walked along Fortieth Street until you saw the single red bulb marking the entrance. Pull open the door and step inside. Upstairs was the bar with the Harleys; downstairs there was a stage in a bare, empty room with another bar propped crazily against the wall. The floor felt like liquidized chewing gum.

There were always little stories coming out of Siberia for Page Six—Jimmy Fallon and Horatio Sanz would sometimes get drunk there, and Tracey always had great gossip about the machinations of the Hell's Kitchen nightlife world. The upshot was that I usually drank there for free.

The thing I really liked about Siberia, though, apart from the free beer, was that no one would bother me in there. No one in that place would criticize me or tell me I drank too much, because there was always someone there drunker than I was. I felt right at home in its dingy, graffiti-covered interior, which reminded me in a funny way of the Nostril, the old bomb shelter we used to smoke in back at Eton. It was almost impossible to get in trouble in Siberia. I only saw Tracey flip out twice. The first time was when I lit a prerolled joint I had in my pocket while I was sitting at the bar, and he went ballistic. The second time was when he threw out some loud investment banker types—all Brooks Brothers shirts and handmade shoes—for swearing. "No cursing!" he hollered as he pushed them out the door. "That's the rules of Siberia!" As he came back in, he shook his head and sighed, "Those fuckin' guys were really getting on my fuckin' nerves."

"Fuck 'em, man," said Chris, and we all spun back to our drinks.

If you got in a bad mood, or a good one, or you just wanted to let off some steam, you could kick a hole in the wall or smash some bottles, and no one would raise an eyebrow. Siberia was the ultimate dive bar, a shabby, shitty, black hole—and it exerted an irresistible, magnetic pull on me.

## –145 DAYS

I woke up where I usually did these days, on the sofa, my sofa of shame. It was around six in the morning. I crept as quietly as I could into the bathroom to be sick, then brushed my teeth and got into bed with Sasha. It was Monday morning, but at least I didn't have to go to work. I tried not to think about the fact that I didn't really have any work.

"Did you have a fun night, Monkey?" Sasha asked me.

"It was okay," I said. "Late, you know. I crashed out on the sofa. Sorry."

"Don't be sorry," she said.

Sasha always said stuff like this, and I never knew what she meant. Was this okay? Or was it that this was definitely not okay and words weren't going to change that? I remembered Alex telling me that sorry didn't mean anything if you just went out and did the same thing over and over again. It seemed like a lifetime ago. I lay there in silence for a few minutes, the morning light filtering through the curtains, sheets of cotton nailed to the wall.

Neither of us was asleep. "Monk, I think I am going to have to stop drinking," I said.

"You don't have to stop," she said. "You just have to limit yourself. You just can't get totally wasted every night of the week."

"Yeah," I said, relieved I wouldn't have to quit after all.

And then I had a plan. "I know what. I'll just drink two or three drinks a night every night. And just get actually *drunk* one night a week." Pause. I rolled up on my arm and looked at Sasha and thought about the week ahead. There was a party tonight and the next night. I'd have to get drunk both nights. "Actually, *two* nights a week. I'll only get *drunk* two nights a week," I said. "Two nights a week is okay."

"Mmm," Sasha mumbled from her sleep. "Yes, Monkey."

That plan worked well for the next two nights. I got drunk both nights.

It went wrong on the third night, when I tried to just have two—or three—glasses of wine and ended up getting drunk again. Ah, well, I thought, as I tried to catch the barman's eye as I sat at the bar in my local pub with Jean, the manager of La Bonne Soupe restaurant across the street. I'd just have to quit. Someday, not now. It wasn't that bad yet. I could carry on for a couple more years.

"Another Jack Daniels, please, Mark," I said.

"Tommy," said the Irish barman, "first off, me name's not Mark, it's Michael, and I've been tellin' you so all night. Second, no, I'm cutting you off; go home to your wife."

The rage exploded out of nowhere. "Fuck you, man!" I shouted at the barman—Mark, Michael, whatever the fuck his name was. "Fucking tell me what to do, you cunt!" I slammed my empty glass on the bar, but it wouldn't break.

He'd disappeared to the other end of the bar and just shouted back, "Mind how you go now."

Jean was on his feet and was saying to me, "Hey, Tom, easy, easy."

"The amount of money I spend in this fucking place, Jean, and that fucking cunt won't even give me a drink."

"Forget it, Tom," Jean was saying. "Forget it. Just go home."

It didn't look like I had any option, so I left. I walked up the block to my apartment and let myself in. Sasha was asleep. There was one beer in the fridge. I found an old bag of coke and racked up a couple of lines on the table.

I was fine. I just wanted one more drink. I'd go to the other bar on Fifty-Fourth Street and get one. As I opened the door to head out again, I heard Sasha sleepily saying, "Monk?" from the bedroom. "Where are you going?"

"Won't be a minute," I said, walking out the door.

I stormed round to Fifty-Fourth Street. The bar was closed, shuttered, lights off. I considered my options. This part of town was dead at night. It was one thing I hated since we had moved from the East Village to midtown. Nowhere to get a drink. I could always go to Siberia.

And then the righteous anger welled up inside me. How the fuck could that asshole of a barman refuse to serve me? Wasn't I their best customer? Didn't I tip the bastard handsomely? I chewed my lip and ground my teeth furiously as I headed back to Fifty-Fifth Street. I walked up to the bar and tried the door. It was locked. I peered in the big glass window—and there they were, Jean and Michael-Mark-whatever-the-fuck-his-name-was, laughing and chatting away. Fuckers.

I banged furiously on the window, and they both jumped in alarm. "Let me in!" I screamed, the rage surging round my system, feeling terrific. "Let me in! I just want a beer!"

Michael turned back to Jean and spoke to him. Jean shrugged. I walloped the window again. It trembled in its frame. "Oy, Michael, sorry I forgot your name. I just want a drink and then I'll go."

He came up to the window and shouted at me through the glass. "We're closed, Tommy boy. It's time for beddy-byes."

I struck the glass with the fleshy part of my fist again. Hard. "Let me in. Please."

"Don't go breakin' my windows now, Tom, for Christ's sake, and makin' me get the police to fetch ya," Michael was saying.

"Okay, fine," I said. "You won't let me in, I'll just stay here."

So I lay down on the ground outside the bar, parallel to the window. It was cold. I actually was in the gutter looking at the stars. He would have to let me in before I died, right?

I don't know how long I was there, seething with anger, but eventually Jean came out.

"Tom," he asked, "are you okay?"

I wouldn't answer. "Tom, it's me, Jean. The bar is closed. I'm going home. Do you want me to get Sasha?"

So the bar really was closed now. Suddenly I felt sober. What the hell was I doing? I stood up. "No, man, sorry. I'm fine. Just fine," I said and shuffled home.

I got back inside, and there were still three lines of coke on the table. Before I knew what I was doing, I rolled up a note and sniffed one down. I was fine. I didn't need this shit. I needed to go to bed. I swept the rest of the coke away with the edge of my hand. I rolled up a joint to calm me down.

Twenty minutes later, I was searching for the white crumbs in the carpet, plucking them out on the end of my licked index finger with a surgeon's precision, thinking to myself, *None of this would have happened if Michael had just given me a goddamn drink.*

## −130 DAYS

It's the morning after my birthday, and the sun's coming up. I'm fifty stories above Madison Avenue, on the roof of my friend Brad's building and off my face. A head-height wall, about a foot thick, runs around the perimeter of the roof space. I am standing on it. *Stunning view of the Empire State Building,* I think to myself. I stretch my arms in the shape of a cross, and I jump up in the air.

Some of my best friends in the world, including James, my old dealer, and another friend, Frank, are visiting from the UK for my thirtieth birthday. It's been months in the planning, and it turned out to be everything I wanted. A fabulous dinner, plenty of wine, and an eightball of cocaine to keep the drinking going.

James's face has gone white. He is shouting, "TOM, GET DOWN! GET THE FUCK DOWN, MAN! GET DOWN! COME ON."

But I'm not going anywhere. I jump up and land on my perch again and grin at their panic. "Come on, man, get up here! It's an awesome view."

I jump up in the air again and again. Up and down, up and down, on my footwide shelf, far above the city. I jump three inches. Six inches. Not quite a foot. A little gust of wind blows thrillingly. I rock back and forth, my arms outstretched, and mock my friends.

"Woooaahh!" I shout, pretending I'm overbalancing, teetering back and forth like a dancing Jesus on the cross.

Now Frank is shouting at me to get down too. James's tone is angry now.

"It's all right," I say to them. "I'm not going to jump off."

James puts his hands over his eyes, falls to one knee, and says, "I can't fucking watch. Get the fuck down, Tommy. This ain't funny."

I laugh. It *is* funny. I look around the roof at the scene of utter debauchery. It must be five or six in the morning, and we've brought a tiny fold-up table up here—it's about nine inches off the ground—to snort coke off. On the roof! There's a bottle of vodka and a bottle of gin. James, Frank, Brad, and I are the last survivors of my thirtieth birthday party.

It really has been one of the legendary nights. About twenty-five of my friends came to Indochine, a restaurant in NoHo, for dinner, then we toured the dive bars and clubs around the East Village, the big package of coke tucked snugly in the small pocket of my jeans next to my keys, which are tied to my belt loops by a green ribbon so I won't lose them. We headed back to Brad's as the sun came up, and now, here we are, on the roof, and I'm jumping in the air.

I share my birthday with my father. I've never observed Father's Day, but because of this coincidence of birth dates, I still get one day a year when I am forced to contemplate my troubled relationship with my dad. I think this astrological quirk of having a mutual birthday is one of the main reasons I am still regularly in touch with my father. I am the only one of all his children who still speaks to him regularly. Once a year I feel like I have to call.

He never calls me. That's just not the way it works with my dad. If you wait for him to call you, you could be waiting a long time. I always call early. That way I can pretend that he would have called me later in the day. Of course he would.

About five years ago, I called my dad on our birthday. I sang "Happy Birthday" over the phone.

"Oh, that's so sweet of you to call," he said, once I had finished. "Thanks so, so much."

I paused, waiting for him to say it. Nothing.

"Oh, that's okay," I said eventually.

*Say happy birthday to me, you fucker.* "How have you been?" I asked.

"Oh, you know, pretty good."

Unbelievable. We were born on the *same day,* for God's sakes. My mom has even told me about the party I broke up by arriving halfway through.

And he can't even wish me a happy birthday. I hate him for this. But I resent him even more for the fact that he never, ever calls me; I always have to call him. I hate him for the fact that he never, not once, ever asks me how I am doing or what I am up to in my life. He never asks, "How's Fred?" or "How's Josh?"

Instead, I say, "Fred's doing well. He's at Oxford, you know." I say, "I got a new job," and I say, "I had a piece in the paper today. I'll send you a copy," but I never do.

When I was fourteen and my parents had separated, I desperately wanted to speak to my dad. I had his address in the south of France, and I sent him a letter from Eton, asking him to call me ten days later at the school phone box at 7:00 p.m. I gave the number for the phone box, and ten days later, I got there at 6:45.

I was sure he would call. I held the handset in my left hand, talking animatedly, with my right hand over the catch so that no one would throw me out of the box before my dad rang.

I had the best conversation of my life with my dad that night. Yes, I was fine, thanks. Upset about you leaving like that, though, of course. Why did you do it? Oh, right, right, I understand. But how could you leave me and Fred and Josh? What about our school fees or anything? Oh, okay. When will I see you again? Oh, really? Oh, great, great, I can't wait.

It was just a shame he wasn't on the other end of the line. At 7:30 I gave up. I lifted my hand off the catch and hung up the handset. I walked back across the road to my schoolhouse as I bit my lip.

I told my mom what had happened, and she told Dr. Harrison. He cornered me one night, saying, "Now, Sykes, I hear you're upset because your father failed to ring you at a telephone box or something?"

The tears started welling up, and I gritted my teeth together. I felt hot, like I was guilty or stupid or had done something wrong. I wanted to deny it. And the way Dr. Harrison was talking to me was so patronizing.

"Come into my office," he said, grinning at me from behind his half-moon glasses.

I stood in front of his desk. He leaned back in his chair. "Well, Thomas, the two things nobody can be responsible for in life are his name and his parents." Dr. Harrison grinned at me brightly, delighted with his witticism. His breath smelled. A tear started rolling down my nose. I swallowed hard. Why was I ashamed?

"There's no need to blub about it, Sykes. It's not your fault."

I turned and walked out of his office, blinded by the reservoir of tears I was trying to keep in my eyes. I couldn't decide who I hated more, my father or Dr. Harrison.

I wrote an angry letter to my father, scrawling out in my fifteen-year-old hand, "Why the fuck did you do it?" and, "You know what I think? I think you decided you just couldn't be fucked."

My dad didn't answer. When I finally confronted him about the letter, he said that I had become "abusive," and so he wouldn't respond.

This I couldn't believe. Now, it seemed, I could talk to my father only in language appropriate for a customer service manager, or I risked getting the line disconnected.

I couldn't face being shut off entirely, so I played along instead. Whenever I would meet my dad, I would never suggest I was unhappy. I only asked him once or twice why he had abandoned me and my family. He exploded in rage and almost walked out of the restaurant we were in each time. I learned to leave it alone. We talked instead about other things, my dad joking and laughing and telling me funny stories about his friends and acquaintances. His car. His new house. His company. It was always his life, I noticed, not mine. He still never asked me a thing.

So my birthday has always been a mixed-up day for me, making a phone call instead of waiting for one that might never come. Best dealt with by getting obliterated and doing something stupid, like jumping as high as I could in the air several hundred feet above the cold, hard tarmacadam.

*Jump.* Forget the fear.

*Jump.* Forget my dad.

*Jump.* If I fell, he probably wouldn't find out for a week or two anyway.

*Jump.* I might be like him.

*Jump.* And every year, on this day of all days, *my birthday*, I have to spend all day thinking about him.

When I was fourteen, I started crying. I cried the whole time. Someone would only have to mention my dad—or *their* dad—and I would feel hot, feel the welling begin. I was embarrassed to be such a baby. To *blub*. It was shameful.

So I stopped crying. I didn't cry for a long, long time.

Eventually I climb down off the wall. James is pleased. He throws his arms around me. But all I can think is that I want to speak to my dad. There's a conversation I need to have with him. I need to just sit down and ask him one very simple question: Why didn't you ever care to see your kids, Dad?

I got home that morning at about seven. Frank and James stayed out on the roof, drinking until after the sun came up, and then fell asleep up there.

It was June, and when they came up to my apartment the next night, they were so sunburnt that they looked like they had been involved in an industrial beetroot juice spillage. Frank showed me where his T-shirt had ridden up his chest while he slept, giving him a ring of livid sunburn on his stomach, which ended just below his solar plexus like a punch line.

"It was totally bizarre when we woke up," said James. "There were two really neat and trim gay guys up there looking at us in disgust. And there were just bottles of warm gin everywhere."

James was punctuating the story with his throaty London chuckle. "I'd cut my foot, and there was blood everywhere. And Frank and me were just lying in the middle of it all, totally passed out. I woke up and I saw these guys and sort of nudged Frank. 'Franky! Franky!'..."

Frank took up the story, trying to control his laughter. "And I was like, 'What?' and I tried to stand up, and my sunburn was just like, Aaarghh!"

We all laughed. Then I said to James, "I can't believe I was jumping up and down on that wall, man."

And James's face crumpled. First it went white. Then he scowled, an expression somewhere between fury, sorrow, and pity. He just said, "Fucking hell, Tommy. That weren't funny."

I'd booked us for dinner at Jean-Luc's on the Upper West Side. He gave us the private room. It took about six bottles of wine just to take the edge off that night.

## -100 DAYS

Chris and I had been invited on a three-day, all-expenses-paid press trip to Amsterdam by Heineken.

"Oh, my God," said Paula when she found out where we were going for the weekend. "You two are going to Amsterdam? With a beer company? Are they out of their minds?"

Well, yes, they were, but they needed coverage.

I had been to Amsterdam a few times as a teenager on weed-smoking holidays. It was easy to get there from London; and although the grass wasn't much cheaper, the fact that you could just buy it in coffee shops and openly skin up right there on the sidewalk was sufficiently novel to keep us going back. As our flight droned over the Atlantic, I tried to sleep, but memories of the city had me too excited to get much rest. I felt the way I often did before a big party—excited but nervous about the potential extent of the mayhem that lay in store.

The first night we arrived, a Thursday, I dragged Chris out to shoot some pool. His bag had been lost on the flight, so all he had was the clothes he was standing up in and a credit card—not his credit card, though; he used Ron the PR guy's. We hit a coffee shop first and got some cannabis. Underneath a glass countertop, there were thirty different types of hash and herbal marijuana. I bought a few grams of *charis*—a particularly potent Indian hashish resin—from the hippie behind the counter and sat down at a table to skin up with a cup of herbal tea. All the coffee shops in Amsterdam have lame names, many of them harking back to 1970s psychedelia. We were sitting in the Doors café, just across the street from the Pink Floyd. If I opened a coffee shop here, I'd call it the Funkadelic and play *Maggot Brain* all day.

The Doors was decorated like a student stoner's flat—drapes on the walls, drapes over the chairs, and maybe a total of about sixty watts of light illuminating the whole place. In fact, skinning up in there reminded me of all those years ago in the Nostril.

I skinned up a joint—expertly splitting a cigarette and emptying the tobacco into the rolling papers, burning the sweet-smelling hash, and crumbling it on top. It smelled vegetal. It was sticky, oily, and I had to rub my fingers to get it all off. I felt the anticipation of the first hit building in my mind. I savored the expectant feeling, rolling it around my synapses like a fine wine. I stuck down the paper and smoothed out the joint.

I lay back on the banquette and stuck the joint between my lips. I sparked the lighter, touched the end of the joint to the flame, and inhaled. The joint crackled like a forest fire.

The first puff of a joint is always the best. I visualized the thick herbal smoke spiraling down my bronchial tubes into my lungs, filling them all with the beautiful, deadly, narcotic toxins.

One second . . . two seconds . . . and there it was. The drug hit my brain, and I was back in the zone. I exhaled a plume of purple smoke. I took another few hits and passed it to Chris.

The Doors café played only the Doors, which must have been tiresome if you worked there, but it was fun to visit. I lay back, my head not spinning so much as revolving slightly, and wondered as I often did what it was that marijuana really did to me. I had smoked dope since I was fourteen and was a regular smoker by the age of sixteen. At seventeen and eighteen, I was buying an ounce and selling seven-eighths of it, getting a free eighth for myself. I weighed it out on an old set of postal scales I had found in the attic at home.

I quit smoking dope three times in my life. The first was when I had to do my A-levels at eighteen (three months). The second was when I had to do my final exams in Edinburgh when I was twenty-two (three months again). The third had been when I came to New York, aged twenty-nine (two weeks). I had meant to stop for good in New York, but once I found out where to buy grass, the quantities crept back up until I was smoking half an ounce a week once again. There had been another enforced interval when I had to get a new dealer because my old one had discovered that I worked for the *Post*.

"Huh, Tom Sykes of the *New York Post*?" he said one day when he came into my apartment and I had left a copy of that day's paper out. "Interesting. Very interesting."

My new dealer worked for another paper across town. An ounce cost me about $100. By now it lasted just over a week.

Chris passed the joint back to me. I lay down on the banquette, stretched out full length, and brought the joint down to my lips. I shut one eye against the smoke and squinted through the other as the tip glowed bright red. A burning lump of hash fell on my face. I hardly felt it but brushed it away automatically. This was some good shit, I thought to myself, laughing at how clichéd I sounded. But then again, I was in the Doors café in Amsterdam, and Jim Morrison was saying, "Out here, in the desert, we are stoned immaculate."

"You want another one?" Chris asked incredulously. His eyes looked like two-day-old fried eggs, and I guessed mine were the same.

Yes, I wanted another one. And another after that. I wanted to sit here all day and get wrecked. Wasn't that what everyone wanted to do? Wasn't that the whole point of being in Amsterdam?

I opened my mouth to speak, but nothing came out. So I just looked at Chris and said, "Uuuh?"

I carried on rolling up. When the joint was ready, I fired it up and passed it to Chris. "No, man, I'm stoned. I won't be able to see. That's enough."

Enough? Enough? What did *that* mean?

I smoked the rest of the joint myself. I sat up on the banquette, but my limbs felt too big for it. Chris had started talking to some people at the table next to us. I wanted to join in, but I couldn't think of anything to say. I moved my mouth, but my voice wouldn't work. I wished I wasn't so stoned. But seeing as I was, I figured another joint might make me feel better. I started sticking together the papers frantically.

"Oh, my God, you're having another one?" asked Chris.

I nodded dumbly. "We've got a lot of weed to smoke over the next few days," I said, waving the bag in front of me, my voice thin and cracked.

Chris stood up. "All right, man. Whatever. I'm going to check out the city a bit." He walked out the door.

I looked around the coffee shop. Everyone else was in twos or threes. I was the only person on my own. I carried on rolling up the joint. I smoked it. I sat there, stoned. My heart was racing. Everyone seemed to be looking at me out of the corner of their eye. I wished I had a newspaper to read. Something to occupy me. An excuse to stay here.

But this was how getting stoned went these days. Stage 1, skinning up the first joint: excitement. Stage 2, smoking the first few puffs: sweet release. Stage 3, actually being stoned for the rest of the day: racing heart, paranoia, feeling incapable of doing anything, crushing depression, smoking more, on my own, to try and feel better and just feeling worse. That's where I was now. I didn't know what to do with myself, but I managed to make it back to the hotel across the road. I crashed out in my room, justifying it to myself by saying that I was suffering jet lag.

When I woke up a little over three hours later, it was getting dark and I felt a lot better. I knew from experience that it took me three hours without a joint to stop feeling actively stoned, although most mornings I still had a cloudy head. Smoked-over, I called it.

I reached out for the phone and called Chris's room.

"Yo," I said when he picked up. "Wanna go hit some bars?"

I was determined to leave the weed behind, but I couldn't resist having one quick hit before I left the room. I met Chris in the lobby five minutes later. Chris was dressed head to toe in H&M, where he had bought an entire holiday wardrobe to replace his lost case. Cargo pants, primary color T-shirt, the works.

"You look like Avril Lavigne," I said.

"I feel like a total idiot," Chris conceded. "But my suitcase still hasn't arrived. I didn't want to spend too much dough."

"Come on, Skater Boy. Let's shoot some pool," I said.

We found a pool table in the basement of a bar, accessed by a particularly steep, narrow, and winding staircase. In the middle of the third frame, Chris went upstairs to get some beers and came back down with a huge crash as he fell down the stairs.

He limped around a bit that evening, but the next day he pulled up his T-shirt and showed me the bruise. It was the nastiest thing I had ever seen. It started halfway up his left buttock and was the size and shape of a rugby ball, spreading up to his kidney. It went from blue to black to green to a deathly yellow. Chris limped around the whole weekend, moaning, "I got a broken ass."

On Friday night, we went to a coffee shop. I got so stoned that during dinner I became convinced that a diminutive DJ called Speedy, who was also on the press trip for a regional radio station, was trying to kill me. "Speedy wants me dead," I kept saying to anyone who would listen over dinner. "I don't know what I've done, but he wants me dead!"

The big party was on Saturday—Heineken was sponsoring an event with the unhappy name Amsterjam. On the bus on the way there, a fat, sweatpants-wearing American woman in her forties stood up in the bus and started officiously saying, "Testing-testing-1-2-3," into her microphone.

"Okay, hi!" she said, holding heavily onto the coat racks as we swung through Amsterdam's twisting streets. "So we are going to Amsterjam, and we here at Heineken, we would really appreciate it if in your stories and broadcasts, you could try and mention the Heineken slogan at least twice. Remember, the slogan is 'It's All about the Beer.' We also would appreciate it if you didn't talk too much about the coffee shops and the marijuana situation."

"Can we mention magic mushrooms?" I asked, shoving a handful into my mouth and pulling a face while I chewed them down.

The festival was actually pretty good. I was buzzing nicely off the mushrooms. I had stacks of weed to smoke, and I found a UK jungle tent where I sat for hours. I shared a joint with some Dutch guys and lay on my back in the sun, feeling my arms stretched out and the sun beating down on me.

Toward seven, with the sun going down, I ran into the fat lady whose main job seemed to be to corral us. When she saw me, she pounced. "Where have you been?" she yelled, grabbing my arm. "C'mon. It's time to go. The bus is leaving now."

"Whoa, whoa, take your hands off me, please," I asked. Everything was happening in slow motion, and I felt very calm. "I'm not coming back on the bus," I said.

"Oh, yes, you are," she said, sweat rolling off her face. "You *have* to."

Whenever anyone tells me I have to do something, I do the opposite. A taxi driver told me I had to use the curbside door once, so I used the one on the roadside instead. I escaped death by fractions of an inch as a blaring eighteen-wheeler jinked past me.

I looked at the fat woman telling me to get on the bus. "Listen," I said. "I love festivals. I get festivals. It's just getting dark, and this one is just about to start. You are crazy to go now. The rubbish bit is just finishing. This is where it gets good. If you want to go, go. I'm staying." I paused.

It's really, really hard to talk sense when you are tripping on magic mushrooms. You can do it for a bit, then you just lose it. So when she asked me, "How will you get home?" instead of saying, "I'll take the train like everyone else," I replied, "I met some Dutch friends of mine. They said they'll give me a lift."

By this time, we had been joined by the New York PR, Ron, who asked me, "Well, where are they?"

I looked around me and looked back at Ron. He was zooming in and out of focus. "Actually, they don't exist. I just made them up." I sighed. "Really, though, I'll be fine. I'll take the train."

Ron tried to argue with me. He was halfway through making his next point when I said, "Look, sorry. Have to go." I ran, ducking and weaving into the crowd until I was lost.

The festival was awesome. I gobbled up mushrooms and beer and went back to the UK jungle tent for the rest of the night.

"Oh . . . my . . . oh, my golly gosh," the MC yelled down the mic. I roared my approval and felt homesick for London. What was I doing here anyway?

About midnight, the festival closed down, so I just followed the crowd to the exits. The Dutch, I thought to myself as I climbed on a train, are so incredibly organized that, really, there had been no need for anyone to worry about me. Heineken might be a bit pissed off, but what the hell? They were the ones who had brought us to Amsterdam, the land of legal drugs.

I got back to the hotel. I was still tripping pretty hard when I walked into the lobby at about two. It was quiet. The concierge behind the desk hardly raised his eyes at me. I was starting to feel a little bad now. I hoped the PR people were not too worried about me. I should call up to their room and say sorry.

I tried to explain to the desk clerk what I wanted, but he wouldn't put a call through for me. Seeing as how I was resting my chin flat on his desk, I can't, in retrospect, really blame him.

But then I saw a board in the lobby with the Amsterjam logo on it and a twenty-four-hour number. I'd call that, let them know I was okay.

The number rang a few times, then it clicked and switched to an American dial phone. A woman four thousand miles away in California, where it was Saturday afternoon, picked up the phone. "Hello?" she said frantically. "What is it? What's the matter? Why are you calling the emergency line?"

"Everything's fine," I said. It was dawning on me that maybe this call wasn't such a smart move.

"Who is it?" asked the lady at the other end of the phone, who was sounding close to tears. "What's happened? Tell me what's happened. My God, I knew Amsterdam was a bad idea!"

"No, really, everything is fine," I said. Oh, shit. This was bad. The woman on the other end of the line was freaking out big time. "I was just calling to say I managed to get a train home to the hotel."

"Who are you?" screamed the woman. "Why the hell are you calling? Just tell me."

"Okay, look," I said. "My name is Tom Sykes. I work for the *Post*. And I stayed behind at the rave, and now I am back at the hotel. I was just calling because it seemed like everyone was really worried about me."

The phone went silent at the other end. "Hello?" I asked eventually.

"Let me get this straight," said the woman, who had now metamorphosed from a sobbing, emotional wreck into an icy block of corporate communications. "You're calling the emergency line to report the fact that *there's no emergency*?"

"Well, yeah, I suppose so," I said. "But, there *could* have been an emergency, right? If you think about it."

"Okay, Mr. Sykes," she said after another long pause. "I am so glad you're okay. Why don't you run along to bed now?"

## −99 DAYS

I woke up in the morning feeling unbearably toxic, dislocated, and spaced out from the combination of mushrooms, beer, and weed.

I'd been awake about two minutes when I remembered the late-night phone call. Why did every single night out always have to end in such embarrassment and disaster? Why couldn't I drink like a gentleman? I stood vacantly in the shower with the water beating down on my back and head for an age as I pondered my stupidity. Well, with any luck, no one on the trip would have found out about it. Maybe the woman I had spoken to had just forgotten about it. Why had I given the woman my name? I bumped my head gently against the tiles and cursed my idiocy.

Eventually I went down for breakfast.

I had just sat down at a table with a glass of orange juice when a guy named Mac, who was another one of the Heineken coordinators, pulled out a chair and sat down at my table.

I stared down at my fruit salad. I wouldn't look up. After thirty seconds or so, Mac asked the top of my head, "Tom, did you call the emergency number last night to report that you got a train back to Amsterdam and were home safe?"

Very, very slowly I raised my head. I met Mac's eyes. They were clear and bright. I knew my own were hopelessly bloodshot, verging on yellow. I was a mess.

I had to look up. "Er, yeah, I did. Sorry, man." I scratched my head apologetically and pulled a pained face.

"Tom," Mac said, fixing me right in the eye with a steely gaze. "I think you are actually okay as a person, and I quite like you. But you are the most ridiculous man I have ever met."

I cracked a smile. He was kidding, right? He wasn't really mad at me, surely?

But Mac wasn't smiling. Not one bit. I tried to ease the atmosphere by asking, "Ridiculous as in funny or in the original sense of the word, as in one who inspires ridicule?"

"The original sense of the word," Mac replied. "The bus to the airport leaves in thirty minutes exactly. That is, unless you would rather make your own way there?"

## −96 DAYS

The thing that amazed me most about Page Six was how little you had to write about someone for them to be ecstatically happy. Chris's write-up of our Amsterdam sortie was a classic of the genre. "We hear that Amsterdam was the place for dance music fans to be at the weekend," he wrote, before going on to describe the festival in about four lines, making sure to mention the sponsor's name. I was pleased to note he hadn't written, "It's all about the beer."

I studied the entry in amazement. "Is that it?" I asked Chris.

"That's it, man," he said.

But Page Six had power. One night I was drinking on Ninth Avenue with Sasha at a place called the Brite Bar, which was right next to Marquee, when the owner, a guy named John Libonati, heard I worked for Page Six. He stopped over at our table and said he'd pick up the tab for our drinks.

"Thanks, mate," I said.

John signaled to the bar to indicate that we wouldn't be requiring a bill. It was a gesture I had gotten used to seeing during my time in New York. John combined the international "Check, please" squiggle with a finger pointed at himself and a half-second eyebrow lift.

"So, you're on Page Six, right?"

"Yeah," I said. "I just do one day a week there. Got any stories for us?"

"Well," he said, "Bjork was in here the other day. She was really nice, had a bit of a party. She's kind of crazy, you know."

I nodded. "Wearing a dead swan to the Oscars was kind of a red flag," I said.

"Well, the next day her assistant calls up and says she has left her coat—it's a fur coat—behind," John continues, "can she come round and get it? So I go look in the cupboard, and sure enough, there it is. So I get back on the phone and say, sure, she can come round any time."

I leaned back in my seat and took a sip of my drink. "So what, Bjork forgets her coat?"

"Yeah, right, but the thing is, a few days after the assistant has been round to get the coat, we get another message from the assistant saying can we please return Bjork's iPod. I call up and say there was no iPod. And then they basically accuse me of having stolen her iPod. I tell them we don't have Bjork's iPod. Then I hear Bjork in the background, going on and on and on about how we have stolen her iPod and want to steal all her music or something. In the end, I just hang up. Five days later, we get a very sheepish message. It's Bjork's assistant. 'Uh, sorry,' she says, 'Bjork found the iPod. It slipped down behind the seat in the car. Sorry about that.' I can't believe she thought my staff would steal her belongings out of her coat! What, did she think we were going to put it on eBay or something?"

By that time, everyone at the table was laughing. And I said, "Yeah, that's a funny item. I'll see what I can do."

The next day was a Friday, so I wrote the item up and ran it on Monday.

On Tuesday, the phone rang. It was John. "Hey, Tom," he said, "I just wanted to say thank you so much for the great item on Page Six. The bar's been packed ever since. And you wouldn't believe the calls I've been getting."

"What calls?" I asked.

"Calls about the story from all over the world. Newspapers from

London to Brazil. And in Iceland, they have gone crazy! Crazy! We've even done telephone interviews with Icelandic TV stations. It's incredible."

It turned out that all the other newspaper gossip columnists in the world read Page Six online every day to get ideas and stories. They'd liked the Bjork item and had run it themselves. Then the really industrious ones had looked up the number of John's bar and called for more details. I checked the Internet while John was on the phone, and there were over five hundred different accounts of my story. "We just stopped answering the phone after a while," he said. "Thanks so much. Come here anytime. We'll take care of you."

"I might just take you up on that, John," I said.

## −89 DAYS

When someone offers you a free drink because you've done something useful for them, it's best to take them up on the offer sooner rather than later, while their gratitude is still ripe. So a week later, when I was out with Sasha and our friends Emma and Jules, I asked, "Anyone want to get drunk for free?" and we hopped in a cab to the Brite Bar. The place was heaving when we walked in, but John swiftly cleared us a table and got a waiter to take our orders.

I was in the mood to get drunk and began drinking fast, even by my standards. I knocked back about five or six cocktails in the two hours or so we were there. It was Fleet Week in New York, when the navy docks in the town. A couple of twenty-one-year-old sailors were standing by the bar looking nervous and out of place, glowing white in their full uniforms. I walked up to them and asked if I could get them a drink as a mark of respect for the fine, unselfish service they were rendering the country. They accepted, of course, and we got chatting.

More than anything, it turned out, they wanted to go to Marquee.

They had read on Page Six that Marquee was a hangout for everyone from Paris Hilton to Ja Rule, and they had come over to Ninth Avenue from their ship, or wherever they were staying, only to be turned away at the door.

I saw an opportunity to be magnanimous. "I'll take you in, lads," I said. "You wanna go now?"

Sure, they said, skulling their drinks and grabbing their coats.

"Then let's go," I said.

"I'm just going to get these boys into Marquee," I explained to Sasha and our friends. "Won't be a minute."

She looked up at me in confusion, but I was already out of the door.

There was a mob of maybe two hundred people trying to get past Rich, the doorman at Marquee. The girls were dressed in tiny strips of chiffon, the guys were either merchant bankers in suits or hipsters wearing vintage AC/DC T-shirts. My two sailors were wearing full uniform—white sailor suits set off by those bizarre round hats.

No matter, I was Tom Sykes from the *New York Post*. I fought my way to the front of the mob and caught Rich the bouncer's eye. He came over.

"Hey, Tom, how many are you?"

"Just three," I said, pointing at the two sailors.

Rich paused for one-twentieth of a second, looked at my seafaring buddies—who really looked very uncool—took a deep breath, and said, "Okay, come on in."

The sailors could hardly contain themselves, and suddenly I saw my world from their perspective. The hundreds of pairs of eyes enviously staring at them as they walked the red carpet into the club. The doorman, who just hours earlier had ignored them as worthless specimens, was now shaking their hands and introducing himself. The people inside the club, waiting to pay their cover charge to get in, wondered who we were as the owner, a guy called Noah Tepperberg, came out to greet us and led us directly into the booming interior, stuffed to the gills with the beautiful people of Manhattan. Once I had them inside, I bade the sailors farewell and zipped back out the door to the Brite Bar. I got back to our table flushed with success and self-lessness.

"What was all that about?" Jules asked me.

"They couldn't get into Marquee, so I took them in," I said. "Military men deserve a break."

We had a few more drinks. We were all slaughtered. Everyone stood up and got ready to leave.

"Fancy going to Marquee?" I asked Sasha when we got onto the street. "I want to check up on my sailors."

"No, I'm tired, Monkey," she said. "I want to go home."

I pulled a face.

"You go on if you want," she said.

I pulled out my cell phone and rang Chris.

"Where are you, man?"

"We're at Marquee," he said, the music blasting out Snoop in the background. "Come on over."

"I'll be there in five," I said, snapping the phone shut. I turned to tell Sasha the plan, but she was already walking away to a cab. *Sod it,* I thought, *I'm going out.*

## −88 DAYS

The next thing I remember, I was in my building, standing outside the door to my apartment. I always carried my keys tied to my belt loops with a bit of green ribbon so I wouldn't lose them. The ribbon had the Paul Smith logo on it. It had come off a box containing a beautiful pink shirt my sisters Lucy and Alice had given me for my birthday.

I was confused. The door wouldn't open. The key went into the keyhole all right, but it just wouldn't turn. I checked the keys. I had the right one. I tried it again. The lock wouldn't budge. Swaying back and forth outside the door, I tried to figure out what was going on. I knew that when the door was open, there was a catch on the side that you could flip down to deadlock the mechanism. Sasha must have activated it. It wasn't the kind of thing you could do by accident. She must have locked me out to punish me for not coming home on time.

I rapped on the door hard with my knuckles. "Monkey!" I shouted. "Sorry I'm so late. Please, can you let me in?"

No answer. No movement inside the apartment. I knocked again, harder. "Monkey, let me in!"

Nothing. I walloped the door hard and shouted again. "Sasha! Come on! This isn't funny. I know you're in there."

*Bitch!* I kicked the door. It bounced in its frame. "Sasha! Please let me in." Silence.

I waited a few seconds, and then I booted the door as hard as I could and yelled for Sasha at the top of my voice. When she still didn't answer, I decided that if she wasn't going to let me in, then I was going to kick the door down. I leaned my bum against the banister and kicked, *Whack! Whack! Whack!*

The whole door was shaking now, and a bit of plaster showered down on the carpet. "Monkey!" I screamed at the top of my lungs. "Let me in or I swear I'll break down the door!"

Nothing.

I gave the door my biggest, most powerful kick, screamed one more time, and then gave up. It could be worse, I figured. At least I was inside, under cover. She'd have to let me in when she went out in the morning. Christ, though, I suddenly realized, tomorrow's Friday. I had to work. *Bitch!* I checked my watch. Five in the morning. I needed to get some sleep. At least it was warm. I lay down on the carpet and dozed off.

I was dreaming that someone was kicking my feet. Then I realized that someone *was* kicking my feet. I opened my eyes, saw three guns being pointed at me, and the shouting started.

"Police! Don't *fucking* move, man!"

I started to sit up.

"Lie down! Don't fucking move! Put your hands behind your head, now, now, do it...DO IT!"

The black holes where the gun barrels ended were all I could see. I stretched my hands up so they were level with my head on the carpet. "What's going on?" I asked. I was so drunk, I swore I was about to laugh. This was absurd. Had Sasha called the *cops* on me?

I don't know how long I lay there before the cops put their guns back in their holsters. There were three of them, and they all seemed short, stocky, and powerfully built.

One of them stepped up over me, his feet on either side of my thorax. "What's your name?" he was asking. "What's your name? What are you doing here?"

"Hi, I'm Tom," I began. "And I live here. I am trying to get into my apartment, but my wife has locked me out because I am drunk. I think. Or else the lock is broken."

"You live here?" the cop said, relaxing visibly. "Where are the keys?"

I started to reach down to my mini jeans pocket, where I kept the keys attached to me, and the shouting started again. The cop standing over me had whipped out his gun, and I actually heard him cock it, *cher-chik*, as all three of them yelled, *"Don't fucking move!"*

The gun was about ten centimeters from my face. I could smell metal and cordite, but still it didn't seem real. I was so drunk, and it was just too weird.

"Sorry, man," I said, lifting my hands up again. I raised them up and down a few times, like I was lifting a particularly light set of weights, and smiled hopefully at the cop. He didn't smile back. I stopped doing the weight-lifting mime.

"The keys are tied to my jeans," I said, pointing with my eyes.

Very, very slowly, the cop put his gun away a second time. He reached down in the same slow motion and grabbed the keys, only breaking eye contact for a fraction of a second. Then he unsheathed a huge hunting knife and with one smooth movement sliced the green ribbon that tied my keys to my belt loop. He tried the door. Nothing.

"See?" I said. "She's done something to the door."

The cop looked down at me pinned against the shit-brown carpet, stepped over me, and walked up the stairs with the keys. One of the other two cops still had his gun trained on me. I heard a *clunk* as a bolt slipped back upstairs. Then I heard him walk heavily down the stairs. He dropped the keys on my chest as he stepped over me. He stopped when he reached my feet.

"You're on the wrong floor," he said. "You live one flight up." I looked at him, aghast. Then he pointed at the door I had been kicking the living daylights out of earlier.

"Your neighbors, who live *here*, called us because they thought someone was trying to kill them. It's lucky you passed out, or you might not be alive."

With that he turned, and all three cops walked down the stairs. The last one turned, looked at me, and said, "You fucking idiot." He said it without pity, without resentment, without humor. Just a simple statement of fact.

I picked myself up and walked up the last flight of stairs. I wandered into the apartment and woke up Sasha.

"Didn't you hear me?" I said. "I had three cops pointing at me. *Three cops were pointing at me!* I could have been killed."

"I can't understand what you are saying, Tommy," Sasha said. "Three cops what? Pointing at you?"

I gave up and walked into the sitting room, lay down on the sofa of shame, and fell asleep.

I woke up the next day at eight, went through to the bedroom, and curled up against Sasha. At ten, my alarm went off—I had no memory of setting it—and I sat up in bed. Shit. It was Friday. I had to get to work.

Sasha stirred next to me. "Tommy, what happened last night? I couldn't get any sense out of you. You were just going on and on about some cops pointing at you."

"Pointing *guns* at me," I laughed. I didn't have a hangover. I felt high. Must have been all the adrenaline still coursing through my body.

*"What?"* Sasha said. "Guns?"

"Yeah," I said, laughing. "I couldn't get into the apartment, and so I was trying to kick down the door. I thought you had locked me out because I was so late coming back. So I went to sleep in the passageway, and the next thing I knew, there were three cops standing over me cocking their guns."

Sasha looked at me sleepily. I was grinning from ear to ear. She said, "Jesus, Tom," and rolled over to go back to sleep.

*All right for some,* I thought. I had to get to work to pay for this high-rolling lifestyle. I jumped out of bed and into the shower and threw some clothes on. I tied my keys back onto my jeans and walked to the *Post*. I didn't have any kind of hangover, although I felt light-headed. I kept replaying the previous night's events in my head over and over again. The funniest bit was the way that the cop had just looked over his shoulder on the way out and said, "You fucking idiot." He'd said it so flat, with no drama or irritation in his voice, just condescension and pity. The way he just tossed it out there made me think I was probably the third or fourth stairwell-sleeper of the night.

It was hot walking down Sixth Avenue. It was going to be a sweaty day in New York. It was a relief to push through the revolving door into the air-conditioned cool of the lobby.

I took the elevator up to the tenth floor and walked down to my desk in the far corner of the office. I sat down in my chair and began firing up the computer and checking my messages, looking for items I could put on the list for the editorial meeting that Richard had to attend in half an hour. I was impatient to boast about my story, but I knew from experience there was no point trying to discuss anything in the frantic half hour before conference.

About midday, as the pages for the weekend were starting to fall into place, the banter started.

"You were drunk last night, man," said Chris. "You were crazy in Marquee."

"What was I doing?" I asked.

"Well, I think you were pretending to do a shit in the flowerpots at one stage. That's when I moved away. It was pretty funny, though."

"Yeah, and you were wasted at Bungalow," said Paula.

I'd been to Bungalow? First I knew about that.

"You won't believe what happened to me when I got home," I said.

"What?" they both asked.

"Well, I couldn't get into my apartment, and I passed out on the stairwell. Next thing I know, there are three cops kicking me awake and shaking guns in my face."

"What?" said Chris, laughing. "You ended up at gunpoint last night?"

"Yeah, man," I said, and told him as much of my story as I could remember. I finished, "And then this cop, he's walking down the stairs, and he just looks at me and says, 'You fucking idiot.' Just like that. It was a heavy-duty night."

Chris was laughing. "That's crazy," he snorted, and we all turned back to our work.

Half an hour later, I asked Paula if she wanted to go for a smoke. Once the doors shut in the elevator, she turned to me and said, "Tom, be careful with that story."

"What?" I said. "Why?"

"Think about it, Tom," she said, sounding exasperated. "If someone at the *Times* or the *Daily News* did that and we found out about it, we'd run it. Embarrass them. Maybe lose them their job."

Her words hung between us in the elevator silence until we pinged open on the ground floor. We stepped out.

"I guess you're right. It wouldn't be that funny then, would it?"

And Paula kind of exploded. "Fuck, no. What—you think it's funny having cops nearly shooting you? Are you fucking *crazy*? And you are going around *telling everyone* about it like it's some kind of funny story? Are you out of your *mind*?"

I puffed on my cigarette, trying to finish it as quickly as possible and get back inside.

The hangover hit me about three thirty that afternoon. I started deteriorating fast. I didn't get a headache, but I began to feel seriously sick in the stomach. I started to see what Paula meant. Being threatened at gunpoint by three cops wasn't funny at all, actually. How could my judgment have been so off? The air was fetid and heavy. I went out to the diner down the block to get a grilled cheese sandwich and a coffee about four, but the weariness got worse.

The problem with working Fridays on Page Six was that we had to do three columns—for Saturday, Sunday, and Monday—and rarely finished before seven thirty. Once we had written the items, we had to wait while Richard edited and laid out the pages in case there were any questions about our stories (which there usually were).

The good thing about Fridays was that Braden Keil, the restaurant writer, would usually open a bottle of wine at about six.

On this particular Friday, I was desperate for some alcohol to fight off the hangover, so when Braden wandered down to our end of the office with a bottle, some plastic cups, and a big grin, I sighed with relief. A few sips of wine was all it took for me to start to feel better. After three or four half-full plastic cups, I was fine.

"Hey, Chris," I said. "You want to go to Langan's for a pint after work?"

"I dunno, man," he said. "I might go home and get some food first." Then he stopped, looked at me, and said, "Hang on—you want to go *out*?"

"Yeah," I said, "just a couple to take the edge off it, you know."

I got to Langan's and stepped up to the bar to order. I didn't have any money in my checking account, so I pushed my British Visa card across the bar. I felt guilty. The house-sale money was almost gone, with just a few hundred pounds left, but sod it, I needed a drink. After a few pints, I started to feel a bit hyper. I had hardly eaten, but the thought of food made me feel sick, and I wasn't hungry. My phone rang, and I looked at the display. It was Sasha.

"I'd better take this," I said to Chris, and stepped outside. I told Sasha I'd be home in half an hour.

At five in the morning, I was racing back from Siberia up Sixth Avenue, trying to beat the sunrise, preparing for another night of broken sleep on my sofa of shame.

## −54 DAYS

My sister Alice was eight months pregnant, and she and her boyfriend, Chris Floyd—Floydy—decided to have one last weekend
away before life, as they had known it in all its carefree, childless
glory, came to an end. They rented a car and took off for a boutique
hotel in the Catskill Mountains. On Saturday night, way out in the
boondocks of upstate New York, three weeks early and displaying
my sister's talent for unpredictability, the baby started to arrive.

I was out at a bar in the East Village, Lucy's, a grungy dive with
pool tables and Formica tables. Sasha was away, so I had been flout-
ing the whiskey ban. I had had a few shots, but I wasn't staggering,
thanks to the contents of the little bag of coke in my pocket.

It must have been about one in the morning when Euan called to
tell me the baby was on its way and asked if I wanted to drive upstate
to greet the new arrival.

"I can't drive," I said. "I'm drunk. Can you drive?"

"Sure," Euan said. "Get a cab over here and let's do it."

I snapped shut my phone. "Hey, Lucy," I shouted to the bar
owner, then I banged the bar and yelled, "Hey, EVERYONE!" The
bar went a little quieter. "My sister's having a baby, and I've got to
go see it!" I put my hands in the air like a soccer player who had just
scored a goal.

Everyone in the bar cheered. I slammed back a few more whiskey and ginger ales on the house for the road. I ducked into the bathroom and had a quick bump of coke to see me on my way.

Euan was waiting in the lobby of his building with his son, Heathcliff, when I got to his place in the West Village. He was piled high with toys and two car seats—one was for Alice and Floydy so they could bring the baby back from the hospital.

It was a freezing October night. We got a cab out to La Guardia airport, where Hertz had a twenty-four-hour car hire depot. While Euan filled out the paperwork, I ducked into the bathroom. The cubicle was big enough to accommodate a wheelchair, brightly lit with a strip light, and had pale tiles on the floor. I sat down on the toilet and took the plastic bag out of my small jeans pocket, squeezed the ends together to open it up, and worked the tip of my small mailbox key—reattached to my belt loops by its knotted green ribbon—into the powder. I raised the mound gently to my left nostril and sniffed as hard and as long as I could.

I repeated the operation another two times, then stood up, flushed the toilet for the sake and sound of appearance, and tipped my head back to inspect my nostrils in the mirror, wiping off a few telltale white crumbs. Then I went back outside to the main lobby, where I danced with Heathcliff to the seventies classics playing on the radio while we waited for his dad to sign off on the car.

Eventually we were off, driving up the interstate toward Kingston, New York, in the dark night. I got another hit of coke when we stopped for coffee and Euan was out of the car for two minutes, and once more at the hospital.

I can't say the proudest moment of my life was frantically trying to sniff a few more grains in the hospital bathroom before I went in to see Alice, Floydy, and their new daughter. I shook my head at myself in the mirror when I had finished, sighed, wiped my nose, unlocked the bathroom door, and floated down the corridor to the desk where Euan was waiting for me to sign in with his little boy.

And so, when I met Scarlet for the first time, I was wired. There was dirt under my fingernails I would never be able to shift. Scarlet was so tiny and clean and perfect and unspoiled. I was afraid to touch her. I had been like her once, I thought to myself as I bent over her clear plastic crib. Scarlet—her soft features seemed to be still forming in front of me, she was no more than two hours old—squinted blindly at the camera flashes. I felt the hot, guilty welling of tears begin behind my eyes and wondered how Scarlet would grow up. Cocaine would probably be a thing of the past. People would shake their heads with amazement when they were told how we used to sniff powder up our noses. There'd be some new, smarter, cleaner drug to get hopped up on by the time Scarlet was eighteen. Then I realized I wasn't eighteen anymore. I was thirty, and I was high in the most profoundly inappropriate situation imaginable.

"Oh, my God, Tom, you're crying," Alice said.

I just nodded, pulled a funny face, and brushed the tears away.

After an hour or so at the hospital, it was time to go. Euan and I bundled Heathcliff into the back of the car and set off to find a place to stay for the night. We found a Motel 6 down the road with two double beds in one room. Euan and Heathcliff slept in one of the beds. I lay sleeplessly in the other bed for what seemed like hours, jealously watching their bodies peacefully rise and fall.

Around seven, there was a knock on the door. It was Floydy. It was whipping with freezing wind outside, so he bundled in quickly.

"Hey, man," I whispered so we wouldn't wake up Heathcliff. "Congratulations. What's going on?"

"Thanks. Everyone at the hospital has gone to sleep. Can I stay here with you?" he asked.

"Yeah, sure," I said, looking around the room with its two double beds. "Er, but you'll have to share my bed."

Floydy was red-eyed, like me.

"Oh, okay, fine," he said. He pulled off his shoes and jeans and climbed into my double bed and fell directly asleep. I waited a few moments, unsure what to do. I was wearing boxer shorts and a T-shirt, the same as Floydy. I looked around the room. Everyone was asleep. I was wired. It was a freezing upstate autumn morning. I climbed reluctantly into bed beside my brother-in-law, trying not to focus too hard on his stubble or the sweaty smell of hospitals and childbirth. I lay there watching the sun come up through the blinds, panicking gently and trying to work out what, if anything, last night meant.

## −40 DAYS

My life continued to gently unravel in the weeks after Scarlet's birth. I still had my bar column at the *Post* and my one day a week at Page Six, but I was having more and more difficulty thinking up and writing the additional features that sustained us financially. I kept pulling money out of my English bank account until one day the screen flashed up INSUFFICIENT FUNDS.

I felt sick, which was all I seemed to be feeling these days. Forty thousand pounds, vaporized in two years. Where had it gone? I had drunk it, I had smoked it, I had sniffed it. I had spent my inheritance on drugs, taxis, and tips. I felt blanketed in shame and stupidity.

I called Euan and asked if he could lend me $500. "No problem," he said. "When can I get it back?"

I said I didn't know. He lent me the cash anyway.

## −16 DAYS

I managed to pay our rent on December 1, 2004, but that was it. I had begged and borrowed all I could. Every time Sasha tried to talk to me about money, I would play down the crisis, roll up a joint to make it go away, or suggest a night out.

I'd only been able to pay the rent thanks to a check from *Men's Health* magazine for a piece I had written about my great-grandfather, Sir Mark Sykes, whom our family nicknamed the Destroyer of the Middle East.

Sir Mark had been the chief British negotiator in a secret deal, called the Sykes-Picot Agreement, with the French government during the First World War to decide how the Middle East—including Iraq, Saudi Arabia, and Palestine—would be carved up once hostilities ended.

But even Sir Mark made me feel bad. You see, he wasn't just a politician. He had fought in the Boer War and written a best-selling satire on military tactics by the time he was twenty-three. When he set off to resolve the somewhat thorny issue of the Middle East, he was thirty-four. I was thirty, and I couldn't even tidy up my bedroom.

## −7 DAYS

The first weeks of December passed in the familiar festive whirl of drunken parties. I had no money and no work. I got up at three in the afternoon, sweated in the bath for an hour, stared vacantly at my computer for another hour or two or wandered into the *Post,* and then headed out to the nearest open bar. I was freezing most of the time because I wouldn't wear an overcoat in order to save on coat-check tips—a trick I learned from watching *The Sweet Smell of Success.* Sasha went back to England on December 9, and I couldn't even afford to pay for a car for her to the airport. She had to get the subway. I went to the station with her so I could help her with her bags.

"What are we going to do, Monk?" she asked me as we said good-bye over the turnstile.

"I dunno," I said. "I'll think of something."

But all I could think about was how much I needed a joint, a drink, and a line of coke.

## −6 DAYS

For the first time ever, I was actually glad to see Sasha go, and all the next day, that realization filled me with disgust. Sitting alone on my sofa, I shook my head and tapped the ash off my joint into an over-flowing ashtray.

The apartment was disgusting. The air was fetid. It smelled of pizza and stale smoke, but it was too cold to open the window.

I tried to analyze my feelings of relief that Sasha had gone. Why was I glad? Was it because the leash was off? Because I could stay out as late as I wanted? Because I wouldn't have to sneak up to the roof for my midmorning joint?

It all sounded logical, but none of that really made any sense. Sasha had never chastised me for drinking. She loved a party, and I knew from our late-night chats that when we first met, one of the things that had attracted her to me was my tolerance for drink: "I used to hate it when I went on dates with guys and they couldn't drink as much as me." She never had that problem with me.

Yet somehow a tremendous distance had opened between us. I was miles and miles away from the shore.

I upset the ashtray, suddenly furious with Sasha for abandoning me. But what did I expect her to do? She'd already made it clear that she wasn't going to play the part of the nagging wife. She had suggested I try cutting down. I had tried. I had failed. I wanted to drink.

Maybe the reason she never confronted me about my drinking was because she hoped, like me, that if she ignored the problem long enough, it would disappear. Maybe she was telling herself, like I was, that it wasn't so bad. That it was just a phase. That we were normal, and everything would be all right in the end.

Late that evening, when I got into bed, I finally realized why I wanted to be alone. It was because I didn't want to have to invent an excuse—to myself or to Sasha—to explain why I didn't want to have sex. Over the past year, I now realized, I had taken to feigning sleep to avoid physical intimacy—either that or stay out all night and sleep on the sofa, which more or less came to the same thing.

We were doomed. How would we ever be able to raise a child? Where would we live? Who would employ me once I was found out at the *Post* and fired again?

The thoughts cycled through my head as I lay there in the darkness. Eventually, I got out of bed, went back to the sitting room, and flicked on the television. A beer, a joint, and Jerry Seinfeld were all the company I needed.

## −3 DAYS

It was a Tuesday night, Sasha was away, and the leash was off; the no-whiskey rule could be broken with impunity. A big ounce bag of weed was bulging in my pocket; and Chris and I, having finished work ten minutes previously, were picking up a dozen beers from the deli on the corner of his block before heading back to his place for a smoke to get the night started.

Chris's skinny midtown apartment was a den of bachelor iniquity. There was trash everywhere, empty beer cans on the table, and a weed pipe on the sideboard. Two massive works by Peter Tunney hung on the wall—a gift from the artist. In Chris's bedroom there was an enormous cardboard box filled with feminine fripperies— cosmetics, underwear, fragrance.

"What's this shit?" I asked him, peering through the doorway.

"That's like my personal goody bag supply," Chris said. "It's all the girly shit I get sent at work. I always tell girls who stay over to grab something from it when they leave in the morning."

I sat on the sofa and pulled the bag of marijuana out of my pocket and set about rolling up a joint.

I took a few hits and then passed it to Chris, exhaling as I sat back on the sofa. We passed it back and forth, and when it was finished, I started piecing together the papers for another one.

I lit it, but Chris declined to smoke any more. "No way, man, I'm done," he said, and we sat there in silence for a bit.

Then Chris pulled out a DVD and said, "But if you want to get high, then we should watch this."

I looked at the case as Chris loaded the DVD. It was a film called *How's Your News?*, and it was a documentary about a team of mentally and physically disabled people traveling around the country doing interviews. In a few minutes, I was in helpless, mean-spirited hysterics at the sight of people with speech impediments, rolling eyes, and limb spasms wandering up to people on the street, shoving a microphone in their face, and demanding, "How's your news?" Most of the time, it sounded more like, "Aaahs yer noooos?"

One guy, a dwarf, had a deliberately oversize microphone with a huge question mark scrawled on it to make himself look even freakier than he already did. I couldn't work out who I was supposed to be identifying with.

After an hour or so, we gathered up our things to head out. No need to discuss where we were going. On a night like this, in a state like this, there was only one option: Siberia.

It was raining, and my feet slapped heavily against the wet pavement as we hurried down Ninth Avenue. When I pushed open the door and walked into the bar, Tracey gave me and Chris a hug and demanded to know what we wanted.

Sitting at the bar, I regretted getting so stoned before going out. I wasn't good for much now. I couldn't really get interested in any of the conversations in the bar, and I was zoning in and out.

Fortunately, I knew a way to break out of my viscous, stoned bubble. "Patrick," I called down the bar, "can I get a martini, please?"

The mathematics of cross-substance inebriation are a complex business. Getting stoned makes you sleepy, but a few drinks wake you up. The only problem is that the drinks eventually catch up with you and make you sloppy. That's when you need stimulants.

By the time I had put away two more martinis, I needed stimulation. I called a dealer's pager number, entered my cell phone number after the beeps, and twenty minutes later, the guy called me from outside Siberia. I went out and climbed in his car, and he said, "Hi—one?"

I nodded, he handed me a bag of cocaine, I passed him $50, and then he was gone.

Half an hour later I was buzzing. Chris was laughing, I was laughing, and I was telling him something important.

"The thing is, man, I always felt like you were my soul mate. And it's not just the booze or the partying. It's just that . . . you get it, man. You get it. I love you, brother. You're a merchant after my own soul. Man, one of these days we'll have to go to rehab together; but until then, man, you know, let's just rip it up and party."

Chris was pretty wasted as well, but not that wasted. He had scowled under his beard when I joked about rehab. "Rehab, man? No way. We're not that bad. At least, *I'm* not."

I shrugged and reached into my pocket to get my cocaine, but my fingertips touched something big and square. I pulled it out and looked at it quizzically. It was the new Ozzy Osbourne greatest hits CD, *The Ozman Cometh*. I'd been sent it at work. I put it on the bar. I asked Patrick to put it on for me.

I loved that tune "Paranoid."

I picked up my martini and took a glug. It seemed a bit weak.

"Patrick," I called out over the long wooden bar, "did you let the ice melt in this or something?"

And then everything went blank.

## −2 DAYS

I woke up the next morning remembering nothing, feeling just panic and pain.

Judging by my hangover, it had been quite a night. Whatever I had done—and I was pretty certain I had done *something*—it had obviously involved a prodigious quantity of alcohol. I had a monstrous, seething abomination of a hangover. I tried to lie still because my head hurt whenever I moved it, my dehydrated brain bruising as it banged against the sides of my skull.

"What did I do last night?" I groaned out loud to myself.

Fortunately, I was a master of hangover cures. The most effective one is simply to drink three pints of water before you get into bed. It's also the hardest to pull off, as the drunkard's appetite for water is reduced in direct ratio to the amount of alcohol consumed. When you have a couple of pints of liquor working their way through your system, the prospect of chugging water for half an hour is not appealing.

So I hadn't drunk my water. Nor had I vomited before going to bed, swallowed any Tylenol before retiring, or even eaten a big, greasy serving of street meat. I had simply crashed out on my increasingly battered and stained sofa of shame.

Most guys only sleep on the sofa when they have had arguments with their wives, but my drunko-pilot seemed to direct me straight to the sofa whenever I was wasted, even on the occasions, like now, when Sasha was away. I had woken there in the early morning and staggered through to the bedroom in the putrid half light. When I awoke for the second time, I realized I was still dressed in last night's clothes.

I tried to think rationally. I rolled gingerly out of bed and ran a boiling hot bath, a real lobster-boiler, and cautiously lowered myself into it. Once my body had gotten used to the scalding temperature, I nudged the hot tap on again with my big toe. I let it run for a few seconds until the temperature was unbearable and then shut it off. A few minutes later, when I was acclimatized, I gave the faucet another nudge with my toe, raising the temperature a few more degrees, sweating out my hangover.

Man, did I feel bad. I groaned out loud. The night was a blank, but I tried to piece it together. I remembered going to Chris's house after work and watching that bizarre video; then, I thought, we had gone to Siberia. I simply couldn't remember anything else.

Eventually I got out of the bathtub and shaved, wiping the condensation off the mirror with every swipe of the razor. I thought I was going to faint. I went back to my bedroom and lay down on the covers to cool off. After twenty minutes, when I had finished actually steaming, I put on a shirt and my Kilgour suit. I checked my appearance in the mirror. I no longer looked like a hungover reprobate. I looked more like a successful—if somewhat pale—nightlife professional.

Walking down Sixth Avenue, I had a bleary flashback to *pretending to be a pinball* on this street the night before. What the hell had that been about? I shook my head at my foolish antics and snickered out loud at the half-memory. I was still kind of wasted. I felt a little dizzy and touched my head and face. It seemed like they were distorted, out of shape somehow.

I walked into the lobby of the *Post* building shortly before five. It was getting dark. *Just another busy day in the life of a bar columnist, right?*

I took the elevator up to the tenth floor and walked to my desk in the features department.

"Hey," said my friend Elysa Lipsky-Karasz, who sat at the desk next to me. "What's going on? Why are you looking so smart?"

What could I say? *Because I just got out of bed and I am trying to hide how hungover I am?* Probably not a good idea. I made up an instant lie instead. "Oh, I just had some meetings and stuff to do today," I said. Then I added, "You know, job interviews, that kind of stuff."

"Really?" said Elysa.

I rolled my eyes and gave her the "shh" sign. It seemed to work. After ten minutes, it was like I had been there all day. Same stupid e-mails, I thought as I deleted my way through them. But one caught my eye. It was titled, "Dinner for fifteen tonight?"

Huh? I opened it up.

"Tom, just checking if you still want a table for fifteen tonight at the opening of Jeffrey Chodorow's new restaurant, Caviar and Banana. We have reserved you the private room, and we are wrapping all the Brazilian knickknacks in bubble wrap in anticipation of your arrival. See you later. Patricia."

Oh, shit. I had completely forgotten that I had planned this—the biggest freebie ever—for fifteen people. And we had a private room as well.

"Hey, Elysa," I called over. "Are you still on for this dinner tonight?"

"Yeah, sure, I'm coming," she said.

I made a few other calls. Everyone seemed to be on for it. I desperately wanted to back out, go home, and curl up in a ball in front of the television, and try not to drink. But there was no way out of this now. I'd have to go. Anyway, I'd probably feel okay after a few cocktails, I reasoned.

I e-mailed the PR. "We'll be there. Nice of you to clear the area. Tom."

She sent back a smiley face. I felt sick.

I'd invited Chris and Paula as well. I thought it would be best to go see whether they were still up for it. I walked around to the Page Six desk and leaned up against the filing cabinet that formed the back wall of their cubicles.

"Yo!" I said. "What's up? You guys still on for tonight?"

Chris looked up at me with a massive grin. "Oh, my God," he said. "Look at you, man! Smart! Nobody would ever know!"

I started to feel the heat build in my cheeks. I looked around uncomfortably, as if he were talking to someone else.

"What, man?" I asked. "What do you mean?"

"I mean last night, man!"

"What?" I said, shrugging the palms of my hands. "What about last night?"

Chris smiled as he realized I couldn't remember. "Don't tell me you can't remember what you did last night," he laughed. "Oh, my Lord!"

"Yeah, man," I said, starting to sweat, starting to feel unsure. "We went back to yours, watched that DVD, and then we went to Siberia."

"Yes, and then . . ."

"What, man?" I said, getting redder and redder and hotter and hotter and hotter. "What?" Paula and Richard were both looking at me with half smiles now. *They'd* already been told what I did. I sighed. "Okay. What the fuck *did* I do last night?" I almost shouted it.

"Dude," said Chris with relish, "*you smashed up the fucking Pac-Man!*"

All the blood in my body churned through my ears with a huge, noisy whoosh and, *bang,* it all came back to me.

I gasped and then swallowed hard as I remembered being Ozzy, the lights in my eyes, singing along. The glass sparkling on the chair legs. And then looking down on myself. Tracey bear-hugging me off the stage.

My head was spinning. Shit. This was not good. Richard Johnson, the editor of Page Six, my *boss* one day a week, for Christ's sake, was looking at me dubiously.

The self-defense mechanism kicked in. *Laugh it off. Say the right thing, and it'll all be okay.*

So I said, "Oh, *that*. I was, you know, just trying to raise the tone of the place a little bit."

Silence.

"Anyway," I said, rubbing my hands with a little too much enthusiasm, "are you guys still on for tonight?"

I was always on for another night.

At the restaurant that night, I cornered Chris.

"Is Tracey pissed with me?"

"Oh, I doubt he even cares," said Chris. "I mean, it's Siberia, you know. It'll just become another one of the legends. 'The night Tom Sykes smashed up the Pac-Man.' Don't worry about it."

"Yeah, I guess," I said, unconvinced.

Chris took a sip of his wine. "Seriously, Tracey won't give a shit, man. Did you ever hear about the night of the thousand shattering glasses?"

"No," I said.

"There have been a couple of them, actually. It's when we just smash up and destroy every single bottle, every glass, every mirror, everything in the whole bar. And like, you know, Tracey joins in. Tracey fucking *starts* it, man. Everything! All the spirits, all the beers, everything—we just smash everything up."

At that moment, Jeffrey Chodorow, the owner of the new restaurant, walked up to me, glaring, and said, "Hey, Tom. Sorry if this place is a bit, uh, 'soulless' for you," and stalked off.

"What was that about?" Chris asked me, confused.

"Oh, I put this item in Page Six that Anthony Bourdain said his restaurants were 'soulless.' So I guess he's pissed about that."

"You wrote that his restaurants were soulless, then overtook the private room for a party on the opening night?" Chris was laughing again. I was not.

I felt sick again, dizzy from the conflation of a hangover and *caipirinhias*.

We sat down to dinner in a large, bare room that had indeed been denuded of all ornamentation. I overheard Chris say to the person on my left, "So, you'll never guess what happened to me and Tom last night?"

I shivered, wondering if this was where my luck would finally run out. I'd gotten away with a lot of nonsense in my time, but this was different. I'd smashed up a bar, for God's sake. Violence, even against an inanimate object, well, that was a new and unwelcome line that had been crossed.

The chatter around the table was lively and loud, but I wasn't part of it. I was zoning out, staring at a wine bottle on the table.

Distantly, I became aware of Elysa shouting, "Tom! Tom!"

I snapped out of my trance, trying to smile, trying to hold it together.

"What?" I said.

"My God, you were miles away," said Elysa. "Are you going out after this?"

"Er, I dunno," I said. I should have gone home. I wanted to go home. But I didn't.

By four in the morning, I was staggering back to my apartment, glad there were still a few hours until sunrise. Tomorrow was Friday. Page Six day. I drank my water that night and got into my bed, not the sofa. I shut my eyes to go to sleep, but I started spinning.

I was back in Siberia, twenty feet up in the air on a thirty-five-degree angle, looking down at myself beating the crap out of the Pac-Man again.

SMASH! *Who is that person?*

SMASH! *That can't be me.*

SMASH! *What have I become?*

## −1 DAY

Somehow I got through that Friday at the office. My head pounded. My eyes, my kidneys, my nose—my whole body ached. I had a metal band around my chest, cramps in my bladder, and shooting pains in my bowel. When I went to the bathroom, my shit was full of blood. That wasn't so unusual, to be honest, but that Friday, sitting on the toilet, staring at the bloody piece of toilet roll in my hand, I desperately longed to be well. I kept knocking back painkillers, but they had no effect. The day dragged on forever. I had a sick feeling in my stomach, and I kept trying to convince myself it was hunger. But when I was in the bathroom, I retched, and I could taste the bitter alcoholic leftovers in my bile. Even worse, I could taste shame.

I needed a quiet night in. I would have gone to see a movie with Sasha, but she was in Ireland. Usually when Sasha was away, we would speak every day; but since I had smashed up Siberia on Wednesday night, I had been avoiding her calls, just sending her vague text messages from my cell phone. I didn't want to scare her.

Late in the afternoon, I rang my sister Alice and invited myself to her place for dinner. Then I went outside. After walking twice around the block and smoking a couple of cigarettes, I took a deep breath and pulled out my phone. On a piece of paper in my pocket, I had scrawled the number of my health insurance company.

With the aid of several deep breaths, I dialed the number. The person on the other end of the phone asked how he could help.

I screwed my eyes up tight and asked, "Am I covered for rehabilitation from alcohol?"

I spent ten minutes on the phone, being passed between various departments. I ended up at mental health. Although I walked farther and farther away from the office, I frequently had to drop my voice because I kept passing work colleagues on the street, and I didn't want them to hear any telltale snippets of my conversation.

"Do you want to make an appointment for an assessment?" a guy on the other end of the phone eventually asked me.

Was I really having this conversation? What was I doing? I tilted my head up and looked at the freezing blue winter sky. Sure, I drank a bit too much, and sometimes I even shat blood, but that was no reason to panic.

"No," I replied, "I'm just asking." I hung up, snapped my phone shut, and went back into the office. I wasn't that bad, was I?

After work, I picked up a bottle of wine on my way to Alice's apartment. It was warm and cozy in her apartment, and her baby, Scarlet, a little over six weeks old, was fast asleep in her crib. We had to keep our voices down. I opened the bottle of wine and poured us both a glass. Alice took one sip and grimaced.

"Yuk," she said. "It's weird, but I haven't really gotten back into drinking since I had Scarlet," she said. "I just don't feel like it."

I was already halfway through my glass. "Good," I said. "All the more for me."

Alice cooked some sausages, mashed potatoes, and baked beans for our dinner, and we watched a bit of television. I felt safe and protected in her apartment, with Scarlet gently gurgling in her cot.

I offered to clear away the plates, refilling my glass for the third time in the kitchen. The bottle was almost done. I gulped back my glass, then just poured out the rest of the bottle.

"So, what's been going on?" Alice asked me as I sat on the sofa with my glass of wine.

"Well," I said, laughing, "I went crazy the other night in Siberia and smashed up the place."

Alice didn't laugh. She looked at me, horrified, and grabbed a hand to her throat. Her whole face went red.

*"What?"* she said, whispering it too loud. Scarlet gave a little squeak. Then quieter, but with the same urgency, she said, *"Tom, what do you mean?"*

"Oh, it's nothing," I said.

I told her the whole story. Well, almost the whole story. I left out the bit about the out-of-body experience. I didn't want to freak her out.

Alice just stared at me.

"Tom," she said, finally. "What are you going to do?"

"Well," I said, "I don't know. Just try and cut down a bit I guess." There was a long silence. I swallowed hard and looked at my feet.

"But, Tom, haven't you been trying to cut down?"

"Yes."

Another silence. So I said, "Actually, I phoned my health insurance people and they said I was eligible for rehab. I could go in for thirty days. You know, quit."

I thought she'd say, "Oh, well, I think that's a bit extreme" or "Don't be silly."

But her eyes lit up, and she said, "Oh, my God, Tom, that would be brilliant."

Maybe I *was* that bad after all.

## −1 DAY (CONTINUED)

I left Alice's house, got out of the subway at Fifty-Fifth Street, and started walking back to my apartment through crowds of drunken revelers careening around midtown as I tried out the word *rehab* on my tongue. It didn't sound right. I felt fine now, anyway.

I hate December. Christmas is the worst time of year for the serious drinker. The bars and clubs are full of idiots in suits who can't take their drink, being sick on the sidewalk after three vodka and tonics. Amateur hour.

I saw Jean from La Bonne Soupe standing outside the restaurant having a smoke.

"All right, Jean," I said, mooching up to him and shaking hands. "How's it going?"

"My God, it has been like a zoo in there," he said, sighing and nodding at the restaurant. "There has been a line outside since four. It's totally insane." He looked exhausted. "How are you doing?"

"Pretty good," I said. "Missing Sasha."

"Sasha is in Ireland still?" asked Jean. "When is she getting back?"

"Next Thursday or Friday, I think, then we are staying in New York for Christmas."

"Are you going tonight?" asked Jean.

"Going where?" I said.

"To the party! There is a Christmas party at the bar across the road for all the staff at the restaurant."

I'd forgotten all about it. Yves, who owned La Bonne Soupe, had invited me to the staff party earlier in the week. I shouldn't go, really, I should go home, but Yves would be disappointed if I didn't show my face. And Yves always had terrific wine at his parties. "It's going on now?" I asked.

"Yes," said Jean. "Right across the street."

I told Jean I would see him there later, spun on my heel, and walked over. There was no way I was going to go to rehab. I wasn't that bad. It was Christmas.

The party was jammed with beautiful French girls and cool French boys drinking wine and dancing to Europop music. I grabbed a glass and started chatting to some of the staff from the restaurant. Someone handed me a package of coke, and I went into the bathroom and poured out a fat line for myself on the toilet cistern. Then I went back to the party and drank more.

The next thing I knew, I was surrounded by four angry Italian-American guys.

"You wanna get fucked up?" one of them was saying. "You wanna get fucked up, just carry on talking, you prick." He was jabbing me in the chest with his finger. "You wanna get fucked up?"

"No," I said, "I don't wanna get fucked up." What the hell was going on? How did I get into this? I had no idea. I must have lost an hour or two somewhere.

"Then just shut up and get the hell out of here," another one was shouting. "Can you do that? Can you just get out of here?" He was thrusting my copy of *The Ozman Cometh* into my jacket pocket. I looked at it, confused.

"And take your music with you."

Uh-oh. Ozzy must have been getting me into trouble again.

"Sure," I said, "I mean, I guess I could..."

I tottered backward on my feet as the guy punched me on my cheekbone.

"Get out of here now!" he was screaming.

For once I was smart enough to not say anything. I just headed for the door, down the stairs, across the road, and back to my house, my cheek throbbing. I had no idea what I had done. What did I do? I pulled myself up the stairs to my apartment by the banister.

Inside, I yanked open the fridge door, grabbed three beers that were in there, and heaved open the freezer, retrieving a quarter-full bottle of Stolchinaya.

I sat down heavily on the sofa and felt something in the back pocket of my jeans crack under my weight. I shoved my hand down and pulled out the Ozzy Osbourne CD, now with a split across the plastic casing. I tried to get up to put it on, but I staggered, lost my balance, and crashed back down on the sofa. On the third try, I made it.

I knew it was late, but I was surprised when the night started to break into another ghastly day as Ozzy kicked off again. I drank my beers. I pulled out my bag of weed and poured all the dry, crumbly herb into a rolling paper to make one last joint.

I poured the vodka into a tumbler. Ozzy was singing "Goodbye to Romance."

Sitting on the sofa at five in the morning with another gray day breaking, surrounded by beer cans and despair, I didn't know what to do anymore. A tear rolled down my cheek.

"This has to stop," I mumbled as I pulled one last time on the joint, burning my fingers and stubbing it out in the overflowing ashtray.

"This has to stop," I muttered as I drained the glass of vodka, feeling the familiar burn of alcohol in my throat.

"This has to *stop*," I whispered as I got up, hit the power button on the CD player, shuffled into my bedroom, wiped the tears from my face, and collapsed gratefully into oblivion.

## DAY ZERO

I jolted awake sometime on Saturday afternoon, and before I had time to register my savage hangover or talk myself out of it, I scrabbled for my cell phone and called my health insurance company again.

"I think I need to go to rehab for alcohol addiction," I said when a person answered. It was a relief to finally say it.

I got funneled through the various departments again, but eventually I spoke to a guy who explained that it would take at least a week to get admitted somewhere.

I couldn't do another week, I told him, and hung up, grabbed my laptop, typed "alcohol addiction quit" into Google, and called the first number that came up.

A gruff Brooklyn voice answered, "Yeah?"

At that moment, all I wanted to do was hang up. I wanted to say, "I'm sorry! Wrong number. I'm just fine! All I need is a cocktail."

Instead, I managed to say, "I need help."

The gruff guy told me that I needed to get to a "meeting" and gave me some directions to the nearest one.

I was willing to try anything, so half an hour later, bundled up against the cold, I stood outside a faceless office building in Times Square. A few dozen yards away, way above my head, on a screen the size of a football field, a giant bottle of vodka levitated, spun, and slowly filled a beaded martini glass. I wanted to reach out and touch it. Yellow cabs flew by me in a blur of lights and horns on every side. A mariarchi band was striking up a tune. Tourists and hustlers bumped past me. It felt like someone was playing a movie in slow motion.

*You could hail a cab right now, be downtown in a bar in ten minutes.*

But I didn't have any money. I turned my gaze away from the massive martini and bundled into the anonymous building with a gust of freezing air.

A security guard sat by the elevator. He looked up from his newspaper and shot me a thin smile as I pushed the door open. He definitely knew.

I took the creaky, piss-smelling elevator up to the third floor and wandered down a deserted hallway to a locked door. A scribbled note on it gave a number to page "if no one shows up."

Great. These people, who were supposed to get me sober, couldn't even manage to unlock a door. I dialed the number and keyed in my digits at the beep. It felt uncannily like calling my drug dealer.

And then I just stood there waiting for the phone to ring, trying not to listen to a voice in my head that was saying, *What are you doing? There's nothing wrong with you. You're not that bad. You just need to tone it down a bit. Turn around now. It's not too late to pretend none of this ever happened.*

Twenty minutes later, bloodshot and shot to pieces, I took a seat in a hard chair the color of shit in a circle of hard chairs the color of shit in a gloomy room made more depressing by futile attempts to brighten it up. Christmas lights. A brightly colored neon clock. God help me.

The seven or so other self-professed alcoholics in the room kept falling asleep—but they got excited when I introduced myself.

"Hi. I'm Tom. I guess I'm an alcoholic. And this is my first meeting ever."

The meeting freaked me out. One guy had obviously drunk so much that he had burned out his stomach. He burped constantly. Another man with a beard, bright eyes, long hair, and tiny sparrow-like features said, "Welcome!" Then he told me he choreographed modern dance. Would I like to come to a performance sometime?

Another guy talked about God. His grace. His will. His power. *Have I wandered into a cult?* I realized I didn't really care if I had. I was so desperate, so bereft, I would have painted a spot on my head if I thought it would help me feel better.

After an hour, they all stood up, linked hands, grabbed mine, and said a prayer.

"God, grant me the serenity to accept the things I cannot change, the courage to change the things I can, and the wisdom to tell the difference."

Before I could make it out of the door, they were on me, pouncing like missionaries. They thrust books in my hands. They gave me cards with their phone numbers, which I threw in the trash as soon as I got out of sight.

One guy with a pink scarf and two plastic carrier bags said, "Call me anytime. I stay up late, late, late."

I said, "Okay! See you!"

The bearded dance choreographer with the bright eyes said one thing that made sense. I had to "count days" until I got to ninety days clean and sober. That seemed like a reasonable objective, I thought to myself as I began walking home. Three months off the booze, and I'd be okay to drink again.

My route home took me back through the middle of Times Square. The giant vodka advertisement had been replaced by a giant Budweiser advertisement. My phone rang. It was Sasha. I let it go to voice mail. Sasha had called three times today already, her messages increasingly feverish and concerned.

This one was no different. "Where are you, Monk? Are you all right? I haven't spoken to you in three days. Why aren't you calling me back?"

I didn't call her back, because if I failed at this, which I was sure I would, I didn't want anyone, not even my wife, to know I had tried.

Traffic zoomed past me in a blur. The eighty-foot sign bleached out my cell phone as it flashed the message "KING OF BEERS" around Times Square. What had happened to me?

## DAYS 1–4

The first days of withdrawing from alcohol were absolutely agonizing, indescribably awful. Sleep without vodka was impossible. A sympathetic friend gave me a few sleeping pills, but they hardly worked. I had to sleep in my bathrobe because I sweated so much at night that I kept thinking I had pissed the bed.

On day two, I sat at my computer screen in my bedroom trying to write about what was going on, when I saw the black shadow of a rat run across the floor. I leapt up in a panic and gingerly lifted up the old towels and clothes strewn across the floor, but there was nothing there. I sat back down. A few minutes later, the rat ran past the corner of my eye again.

"You're imagining it," I said to myself. Then little black bugs started to scuttle across the white walls.

I checked the Web to see what was going on and found my answer. "Alcohol hallucinosis," I read. "This symptom usually begins 12–24 hours after your last drink and may last as long as two days once it begins. . . . It is common for people who are withdrawing from alcohol to see multiple, small, similar moving objects. Sometimes the vision is perceived to be crawling insects."

That night I lay in bed and shut my eyes, but the hallucinations found a way through. Sudden, loud noises like someone was beating a drum in my ear forced me upright in the night, sweaty, swallowing hard, and staring, desperately searching for the light switch.

On day four, I took a good look around my apartment. The place was still drunk. Alcohol containers were strewn across the floor, overflowing out of the bin, littered under the bed. The washing up in the sink was alive. A thin film of filth covered everything. I had to tidy up.

The worst part was finding all the half-empty bottles of alcohol. It was like the end of a party when all that's left is the seriously gross stuff—Green Apple Pucker, Blue Curacao, fruit liqueur, even some Slivovitch from a trip to Eastern Europe. I poured one after the other down the sink in a trance, my mouth watering as I smelled the fumes.

In an ashtray, I found an old joint. The paper holding it together was stained brown with tar that had coalesced where the paper had been licked down. And I thought, *Well, what the hell.*

I looked for a light, but I couldn't find one, so I fired up the gas hob. I lit the joint and pulled back from the flame when I heard a crackle and smelled my hair burning. I inhaled deeply on the joint, holding the smoke in my lungs until I thought I was going to burst. Then, ahhh, exhale.

I got maybe five puffs out of the joint. When I stubbed it out, the first thing I thought was *I'd kill for a drink.*

I sat down on the sofa, on my hands, but the craving kept coming at me.

*This is all a mistake. I'm not an alcoholic. And if I am, I don't care. I'm not like those other bums. I don't drink vodka outside the Port Authority. I drink Dirty Martinis at Bungalow 8. I'm different. I'm a writer. I'm supposed to be a drunk. Did Hemingway ever quit? Or Bukowski, for God's sake?*

I got up and headed for the door. *I'm going to go and get drunk,* I thought. As I was walking out the door, I decided to call one of the numbers I had been given to let them know I was giving up. I talked about smoking the joint with the guy who answered. I told him I was about to go and get drunk.

He said, "You're doing so well, though. You just need to wait till the joint wears off. Three hours maximum." How did he know about the three hours thing?

"Can you hold out for three hours?" the guy said. "If you still want a drink in three hours, I won't try and talk you out of it. Do you want me to come round?"

*No, thank you very much, I don't want you to come round, you pathetic freak. Don't you have anything better to do with your sad and lonely life?*

"No, you don't need to come round," I said. "I'll give it three hours."

I continued manically cleaning my apartment for the next three hours, and in an old file, I found a gold pocket watch my dad had given me for my wedding present. I thought I had lost it years ago. I stared at the watch for twenty minutes and thought about my dad. I wanted to cry, but I couldn't. All my emotions seemed to have been cauterized.

The guy rang back.

"Hey, Tom, how's it going? Still want a drink?"

"No," I said. "Do I have to start counting days again?" I asked.

"Up to you," he said. "Some people would say no, this is just about alcohol. If you want my opinion, I think you should. My opinion is that you can't be high and sober at the same time, but that's just me."

"But if I have to start counting days again, then why didn't I just go and get drunk?" I shouted, furious as I realized what I had been denied—for *nothing*.

"Do you want to be drunk now?" he asked me.

"No," I said. "I don't want to be drunk now."

Silence.

"I'll start counting days again," I said.

"Okay," he said.

I was angry when I hung up. I felt like a child. I got into bed and lay there, just watching the digits on the clock advance toward meeting time, 10:30 p.m. I went to the meeting that night and said, "I have today. Well, this afternoon. A couple of hours, really. I smoked a joint." I paused and then said, "I had *four days*. I can't believe I have to start counting days again."

The room exploded into laughter, and for a few seconds, I burnt with embarrassment and hatred and rage. Then I started to laugh as well, big huge, gasping laughs that sounded more like sobs and slowly but surely turned into them.

## DAY 1 REDUX

I eventually pick up the phone when Sasha calls for the third time on my second first day. She is due back in New York the following day anyway, and I think it might be best if she has twenty-four hours to take in the news.

She says, "Monk, where have you been? Why haven't you called me back?"

I reply, "Er, I've got something to tell you."

"What?" she demands. "What is it? What's going on?"

I begin to blush and feel stupid. *I don't want to be boring.* I feel like I am betraying myself and my marriage and everything I ever stood for when I say, "I've quit drinking."

"Oh, my God, what happened?" she asks.

And so I tell her. I tell her about the Pac-Man machine. I remind her about the money running out. I don't tell her about getting punched, but I do tell her about the despair. My hands look thin and frail as I talk. I have turned from red to pink to translucent white and finally to a ghastly green. I feel green inside.

"Oh, my God," says Sasha again. She sounds totally freaked out. Her voice is thin and frightened. I can't tell whether she's scared by the stories or the stopping-drinking part.

There's silence for a few seconds, then Sasha says, "I feel so guilty not being there to support you. I'm going to get on a plane now and come back tonight. I don't care what it costs."

"No," I say, "don't. You don't need to do that. I think it's good I did this while you were away anyway. I can't wait for you to get back, Sash, but I think this is something I have to do myself. It's a solo mission."

Sitting on the sofa watching a DVD the next afternoon, just trying to get through the day, wondering how Sasha is going to handle it and how I will get through Christmas, my hands wander over my shoulder to feel my back. It is covered in boils—angry, painful swellings rooted deep below the surface of my skin. Although they hurt to touch, I can't stop prodding and pushing them, forcing them to the surface. I run a bath and sit in it for hours, trying to squeeze them. Eventually one explodes with an orgasmic, evil burst of pure pain. I inspect the sticky yellow goo on my fingers. Even from a distance, it stinks of sourness and decay. I am disgusting, but I console myself with the unrealistic hope that maybe my body is beginning to expel some of the toxins that have accumulated over the years.

Sasha arrives late that night. I run down the stairs when she buzzes, kiss her, and carry her suitcase up the stairs. I am trying to look caring, responsible, in control, considerate, like I am getting better. In fact, the effort just exposes how sick I am—despite the freezing cold night, the exertion soaks my T-shirt with foul-smelling sweat.

Sasha wants to talk, but I don't know what to tell her. I try to fill the time with activity instead. I go across the road and get some soups to take away.

We sit down to eat, and I can't put off the conversation anymore.

Sasha says, "I think it's really amazing what you are doing."

I squirm uncomfortably, afraid I am not going to make it even to seven days, let alone ninety.

"Are you freaked out?" I ask.

"No," she says, smiling, holding my clammy hand. But I can tell she's lying. Of course she's freaked out. She's probably thinking some of the same things I am thinking. *Is our life over? Can I do this? Am I going to be boring from now on? Are we ever going to have fun again?*

Neither of us knows the answers.

"I'm going to go out in a bit," I say. "I'm going to go to a meeting."

I spend the next week sitting up late in a diner with some of the crazy people I have met in the meetings. I stay out late, just eating, eating, eating. I know Sasha is at home, confused, baffled, but I can't go back there right now. I have to eat.

One guy tells me that when he got sober, he ate three Indian takeouts a night every night for two weeks. He is thinner than David Bowie. "Just do what your body tells you," he says. I reflect that I have hardly eaten at all for the past five years. Maybe my body is playing catch-up. I don't know anymore.

Basically, I feel like death. I know just how much trouble I am in when I get home that night, climb into bed, and Sasha tells me, in all seriousness, that I look better than I have for years. "I'm so proud of you," she whispers. "I'm so excited about the rest of our lives together."

I am consumed with dread that I won't make it.

## DAY 12

Christmas comes and goes. It's like it's happening somewhere else. My mom visits New York, and we have lunch. We go for a walk down the river, and I just tell her, "I'm not drinking."

She starts telling me what a good thing that is because of all the sugars liquor contains. I feel angry, but I manage to laugh to myself. I don't want to get into it. I love her too much. But I do say, "Mom, it's not the sugars. It's the alcohol."

I keep going back to the meetings because I love the applause. I stick my hand in the air and holler, "Hi. My name is Tom, and I am an alcoholic. I have twelve days." Applause. Cries of "Keep coming back." I sit rocking on my chair, trying not to think, just letting my mind run.

I lie sleeplessly in bed until eventually I turn on the light and scribble on a piece of paper, "If I don't drink, who will I be?"

I don't have any answers.

## DAY 40

I feel good. My skin looks great. The boils are going. In fact, it's hard to believe I ever had a problem at all. *Maybe I am not an alcoholic. Maybe I made it all up. I'd love a drink.*

I do the math to keep myself focused. The first five or six years of my drinking, from age fourteen to nineteen or twenty, I probably averaged about four drinks a night, maybe a total of some seven thousand drinks. The last ten years of my drinking, maybe ten a night. Is that fifty thousand drinks? I could work it out, but really it means nothing to me.

Over the next few weeks, dramatic improvement gives way to steady progress. I wake up in the mornings without a hangover, for example. I feel like I am writing better than I ever have in my life—although I don't have much work. I had to go into the *Post* to tell Faye about my little problem and explain that my days as a nightlife writer are well and truly over.

Faye's amazing. She wishes me good luck. She tells me that newspapers are full of raging alcoholics. She tells me she'll find me other work at the paper. She says, "I didn't know you had a problem with alcohol, but it figures. It makes sense."

"Why?" I ask.

"Well, your work was always so inconsistent. Sometimes it was terrific; sometimes it was just a mess."

I nod my head sadly.

I don't drink, and I go to meetings, two, even three a day. It helps to be around people who have been through what I am going through and much, much worse. A lot of them wound up in mental institutions.

One guy took so much coke, he thought he had bugs under his skin and cut open his shoulder to get them out. Another guy was in the Iraq war, where he got hooked on prescription drugs they called combat cocktails. His two best friends got their heads blown off while they were standing next to him. There's a woman who spent years in destitution collecting empty bottles and cardboard in Bolivia to pay for moonshine. Another lady slept in old refrigerators. A musician reminisces how he could never have less than $6,000 of heroin in his possession at all times. "Just in case," he explains, and we all nod.

But as I start to feel better, it gets complicated, because I want my life back. I don't want to drink, but I do want to see some of my friends. And now I am going to do just that.

Four of the guys—James, my old dealer; Olly, my best man; my mate Frank; and Tom Craig, the photographer I lived with above the kebab shop in London after university—arrive in New York for a reunion planned long before my decision to quit. I manage one cranberry-juice-fueled night out, but the next morning, Sasha and I pile them all in the back of a Mercedes G-Wagon and drive to Vermont for a few days of skiing.

They are so hungover that the whole car stinks of booze. They have hardly been to sleep. I feel *so* jealous.

One night, they want to go to the pub, so I drive them a mile or so up the road, go back to our apartment with Sasha, and pick them up at midnight. I feel like my mother.

On the last run of the last day, I sit on the ski lift with Tom. I congratulate him on how well his career is going. He turns to me, the snow whipping across our faces, and says, "I think what you're doing is so fantastic. It's a real lesson in getting the most out of life. I'm proud of you, big man."

I pull my goggles down so he can't see my tears.

But there's still that little voice, telling me that maybe, maybe it would be okay. Just one last time.

## 90 DAYS

I get ninety days clean and sober. I invite my sisters and some friends to a little party. Sasha bakes a chocolate cake. She decorates it with M&Ms spelling "90!"

The first surreal moment comes when my friend Vivien, whom I haven't seen for a year, calls quite by chance to say he has just landed in New York from Australia. Come round, I say, I'm having a sober party.

"You *what*?"

"I'll explain when you get here."

Then *another* friend, Piers, whom I have not seen in maybe two years, calls. Randomly, *he* has just landed in New York from London. Come round, I say, I'm having a sober party.

"You *what*?"

"I'll explain when you get here."

And I try to explain to them. I try to explain what happened. I tell them the story about Ozzy and the Pac-Man. The trouble is, it sounds like fun.

## DAY 91

I am watching my fingers emptying out cigars and filling them with sticky green marijuana as if they belong to another person. I smoke joint after joint. I down glass after glass of red wine. My teeth turn red. My head spins. *Guess this is what they mean by a relapse!*

I can't work out whether I feel happy or sad. I know I felt happy for about the first five seconds, but now I am not so clear. What is happiness anyway?

I wander into another room, and Alice is in there, crying. That's typical, that she should be there at the same party as me, like some guilty conscience. Her face is red and puffed up. "What are you doing, Tom?" she sobs. "What the *fuck* are you doing?"

"Fuck you!" I shout at her and throw my glass at her. Her face melts into the wallpaper, and I wander back into the main room. Everything has been moved around. I can't find the bar, but a jumble of voices asks, "Fancy another one, Tom?!"

Why not! And another and another! And then I am falling, falling, falling.

## DAY 92

I wake up the next afternoon, groaning in pain, racked with guilt, looking for the blood on my hands.

It takes a few seconds before I realize I haven't been anywhere. The whole thing has been a dream. I laugh like the maddest of the mad Port Authority drunks when I clock it. I have been warned about these "using dreams." I thought they might be fun—not a nightmare like that.

As I make my way to the bathroom, congratulating myself on the fact that I hadn't actually been at a party the night before, I notice something very unexpected. I have a throbbing headache. It takes me just a few seconds to identify exactly what that oh-so-familiar sensation is.

I have a hangover.

I've lived a lifetime of good, bad, and ugly, ugly, ugly hangovers. This phantom hangover is not one of the fun, innocent ones, where we had all crawled out of bed after a house party and fried sausages and bacon, sat round the kitchen table swigging coffee, laughing at the previous night's outrageousness, and smoking joints until it was time to go out again. Neither is it a suicide-inducing, lie-in-bed-and-don't-move number. It is just your regular, horrible, nothing-funny-about-that hangover. You know the kind—the dry mouth, the dull ache just underneath the crown of your head, the mossy tongue.

I figure that despite the fact I haven't been drinking, I need to tackle this like any other hangover. I run a hot bath and sit in it, gulping ice water. I shave. I put on a Paul Smith shirt and a Kilgour suit. I cross the road to the noodle store and order a large bowl of extra-spicy ramen, washing it down with Advil. I feel a little better. But just like a real hangover, it doesn't really leave me all day. My hangover cures, I belatedly realize, were all bullshit, because a hangover isn't just a headache or a sick stomach. A hangover is the physical expression of despair. And all the ramen and Advil in the world can't shift that.

A new guy walks in to the meeting that night. Says he wants to stop drinking. At the end of the meeting, I pounce on him, give him my number. I tell him to call anytime. I tell him I stay up late, late, late.

## 330 DAYS

The days turned into weeks, the weeks turned into months, and just before the months became a year, Sasha got pregnant. Staying away from drink and drugs suddenly became more important than ever. So it was that I found myself sitting at my desk in my apartment in New York one Tuesday afternoon writing a list of my "resentments"—all the people I hated and why I hated them. This, I had been assured by my sober friends, would help me stay clean.

"Dad," I wrote at the top of my list. "He abandoned me when I was fourteen. Never calls to see how I am; I always have to call him. Never in contact with me for sixteen years since then unless I initiate it. Never explained why he left."

I dropped my pencil and rubbed my eyes in despair. This was useless. I already knew I resented my dad for having left my family. This was the *great trauma* of my life, after all.

And it wasn't like I was the one at fault. I had made an effort to see my father once or twice a year. When people asked why I bothered, I would tell them that it was so, when he eventually died, I would be able to go to his funeral with a clear conscience. But really, I knew, it was just because I liked hanging out with my dad. I could bask happily for hours in his intelligence, his wit, and his charm. It was fun, as long as I didn't expect any answers, as long as I didn't say,

"Why, Dad? Why did you do it? Why did you walk out on us?"

Well, now that was going to change. I got up from my desk and went into the other room to find my telephone book. I opened it to "S" and found his number under "Mark Sykes." I went back to my desk and dialed it.

"Hello?"

"Hi, Dad. It's Tom."

"Tom! Hello there."

We chatted for a few minutes, and then I screwed up my eyes, took a deep breath, and asked, "So, Dad, I am calling because I want to see you. I've got some questions I need to ask you."

"Right . . . ," he said.

"Well," I said, "it's been sixteen years since you and Mom separated; and, you know, it's ridiculous we can't talk about it. I need to ask you about it."

"Of course," said my dad. "Anytime."

"Well, how about now?" I asked.

"Now?" he said incredulously. "No, I don't think so. Not over the phone. But maybe we could get together next time you are over?"

"Okay," I said. "It shouldn't be too long."

I hung up the phone, logged onto the Internet, and booked a flight back to London for the weekend.

I e-mailed Dad right away. "How about next Tuesday?"

He shot back, "Fine. Let's talk details nearer the time."

## 337 DAYS

The following Tuesday was drab and gray in England. I followed my dad's instructions through winding village lanes to a pub in rural Oxfordshire a few miles from where he was living. As I drove through the countryside in my rental car to meet him, I wondered what the hell I was doing. What was I hoping to achieve? I prayed that at least I would have the courage to ask the questions that I had wanted to ask for so long, even if I didn't get any answers.

I was annoyed that Dad wanted to meet in a pub. I wanted to be somewhere private. I turned my car into the driveway of the bleak old stone pub and parked. I was ten minutes early, and Dad wasn't there yet.

I went inside and waited.

I ordered a Coke at the bar and wondered what he would say. I fantasized that he would choke up with tears and say, "Well, the thing was, Tom, I wanted to see you so much, but I had a nervous breakdown, and I felt so guilty I just couldn't do it." Then I would start to cry as well, and he would throw his arms around me and sob, "I'm sorry. I'm so sorry," and then I could forgive him.

I shook my head in disgust at myself. *You still think he can wave a magic wand, say the right thing, and make it all better.* My hands were damp with sweat.

Bang on time, Dad pulled up outside. I watched him get out of the car and walk toward the pub. As he came through the door, I hugged him hello as usual. He had a pint of lager, and I stuck with my Coke. We engaged in ten minutes of the usual desultory chat.

"I really like gloomy pubs like this," he said. "The gloomier, the better."

"You would have loved this place Siberia," I said.

Dad finished his drink and said, "Right, come on. Let's go."

"Where?" I asked.

"I have arranged a delicious luncheon at my house," he said.

I grinned. Maybe we were going to have this conversation after all. I got in my car and followed him to a quaint stone village where he was living in a converted stable in someone else's garden.

"My business associates keep telling me I should move somewhere grander, somewhere with a dining room, but I like it here," he said unconvincingly as he let me in. There was a sitting room, with a coal fire going in the fireplace, two bedrooms off to the side, and a virtually unused kitchen with a table littered with prescription drugs. In the sitting room by the fire, there was a table covered in cold meats like chorizo and smoked salmon.

"There's also an attic room with dead bats in it," Dad laughed. He asked me whether I wanted Pellegrino to drink. As he opened the door of the fridge, I noticed it was stuffed with about a dozen bottles of champagne. Dad always drank champagne.

"Enough champagne?" I asked.

"One always likes to keep a little on hand in case of emergencies," he chuckled.

In the main room, my eye was immediately drawn to the paintings on the walls. I recognized them from my childhood. There was a pair of elegantly framed, oval-shaped oils of our ancestors Sir Christopher Sykes and Lady Sykes and a big gold oriental painting that my dad said was a wedding present to his father from Harold Acton. This seemed probable, as my grandfather, Christopher Sykes, was a famous writer who had counted as his friends literary giants such as T. S. Eliot and Evelyn Waugh. He had even written Waugh's biography.

"And the boy on the horse?" I asked, pointing to another familiar image.

"He was a present to my father from the guy who reinstalled the Shah in Iran," Dad said. I could picture it in his office twenty years ago.

We sat down to lunch. I kept sneaking glances at my father across the table. He looked pretty good, but puffy around the cheeks and ears. He told me that he was taking steroids for an inflammatory condition he had developed. The previous Christmas, he had been so badly immobilized that he couldn't even get out of bed. His wife, Sandy, "the Fourth Mrs. Sykes," as he called her, had had to come down to Oxfordshire from London, where she lived, to help him.

The steroids had fixed all the immobility, but they were causing "terrible mood swings."

"Why do you and Sandy live apart?" I asked.

"She prefers it in London, and I prefer it in the country," he said.

We chewed chorizo in silence for a little bit until eventually I said, "So, I want to ask you some questions."

"If you look in the fire there, you will see that there are two potatoes wrapped up in tinfoil baking away."

"When did you put them in?" I asked.

"Before I went out. About thirty-five minutes ago."

"I don't think they'll be done yet, Dad," I said, and then, before he could divert me again, I asked him how much he drank.

"Well, I don't normally drink in the day. Today is different, but of course *many* days are different," he laughed. "In the evening, I would have the equivalent of a couple of beers and half a bottle of wine. And that's not a lot, I don't think. Maybe that would sometimes slip over into two-thirds of a bottle."

I asked him if he considered himself an alcoholic, and he replied, "Certainly not. Of course, I have frequently drunk far, far, far too much on a regular basis. But if you don't *need* a drink before ten in the morning, you are *perfectly* all right."

I remembered when I thought that was what an alcoholic was— someone who had to have a drink in the morning. Over the past year, I'd heard a better definition: that an alcoholic is someone who, once they have one drink, develops an overpowering craving for another. At times, for example, Sasha had drunk as much as I had. But when she wanted just one glass of wine, she had just one glass of wine. I don't think I ever had just one glass of wine in my life.

Dad's tone was light and flippant, and he was starting to relax. I quizzed him further about his alcohol consumption and about the drinking habit in our family. Easy stuff. Then I moved up an emotional gear.

"I came over especially to see you," I said, my heart beating faster.

"I also cancelled something," he said. "I was going to go to Baghdad this week to take part in a debate about Iraq."

I raised my eyebrows inquisitively. "Iraq?"

"I think they might think I actually am *Sir* Mark Sykes, the destroyer of the Middle East," he said. "I do want to go there, though. It's such a great opportunity to see such chaos. Chaos is good, isn't it?"

I didn't have a chance to answer.

"I saw some horrendous things in Algeria in the late fifties. The things the French Foreign Legion did. Atrocities, atrocities, atrocities," he sighed.

This was the story I remembered from my childhood. Late one night, Dad had told me how he had seen babies speared by bayonets to the doorframes of every house in an Algerian town. I had burst into tears.

"It was 1957, and I was twenty," Dad continued. "I had dropped out of Oxford, and I started a club in London called the Whisky a Go-Go, which is still around. It's called the Wag Club. We opened this club for £4,000. It was an unbelievable success, and we got the money back in two weeks.

"By the time I was twenty-two years old, I had all this *money*. I went to Tangier. I got this job—not that I needed a job, but I got one anyway—as a gopher for the Time-Life people there, covering the Algerian war. We saw the dead babies. That was in 1959."

He paused frequently as he relayed his potted life story to sip from his glass of wine. "In 1962 I was living in Paris with my first wife, Helen. I went to Australia with her in '63 and '64, and I made a lot of money in Australia in the illegal gambling business. That's what I was doing in London before I left. I controlled all the illegal gambling in Australia. We were doing it in a classy way, with nice girls, nice food, all that sort of stuff."

"When did you marry Mom?"

"We got married in 1968. Shortly after all this."

"And you were happy for quite a long time, right?" I asked.

"I should think we were basically happy until the money ran out," he said. He paused for a few moments. "Money, make no mistake about it, money is unbelievably important. It doesn't matter when you have it. It certainly does when you don't have it."

And then suddenly, it went quiet, and I squeezed all my courage into a ball in my chest.

*Here goes. What's the worst that could happen? He'll get angry? He'll throw me out? Tell me he never wants to see me again?*

"Look, Dad," I said, "sixteen years down the line, I don't care why you and Mom separated. That's between you and her. . . ."

"If you want a baked potato, you will see a pair of tongs there. . . ."

"Er, okay." *If I don't have the courage to ask this, nothing will ever change.*

"What I was really wondering is why I never heard from you for so long. One moment you were this amazing dad, and the next . . ."

Dad was ready. "I was asked to stay out of it. I was told it would be a very bad thing if I stuck my nose in and communicated with you, and quite wrongly I accepted this."

At that moment my cell phone went off. I cursed as I dug it out and switched it off.

"Potato?" my dad asked.

"I don't think they're ready yet," I said.

"Okay, well, I am going to leave that up to you," he said.

I pressed on. "What about Fred and Josh? Don't you ever want to know what's going on with them?"

"I don't think it's my place to initiate things. I don't. Because I said

I wouldn't. If something is initiated, then wow, fantastic," he said.

*I've been initiating contact for sixteen years. Why didn't you call me on that pay phone at Eton when I was fifteen?*

Then he said, "There's something else which I want you to tuck away at the back of your mind. When I die, my affairs are reasonably complicated. My will is going be lodged at the Central Registry of Wills, and I am going to be making you the executor."

I paused, wondering how much my dad might be worth, then cursed myself for the thought.

But one thing about my father's eventual death had been bothering me for years. Now seemed a perfect opportunity to ask about it. "When you die, how will I find out?" I asked.

He repeated slowly, "Central Registry of Wills, okay. It's all there."

"Yes," I said, irritated that he thought I hadn't understood. "But how will I know you are actually *dead*?"

"How will you know I am dead?" My dad roared with laughter. "Well, I suppose it is quite possible someone could find me here...." He pulled a death-mask face, groaned, and sat back in his chair with his limbs starfished, simulating rigor mortis.

"But shouldn't your lawyer have my phone number?" I asked.

"Well, yes," my dad said. "But how would my lawyer know I was dead?"

We both laughed. Then there was more silence.

Eventually I said, "So you were told, 'Stay away,' and you stayed away? That's it?"

"Yes."

This must have been the first and last time Dad ever did what he was told. I said, "Weren't you curious, though?"

"Yes, of course. But what's the point in being curious about something if you aren't going to have an answer? And you know, I had so many *things*—some good and some bad—passing. Like getting cancer twice, which was very tiresome and quite death-inducing. Like building one amazing business, selling it, and suddenly being a couple of *million* ahead. I thought, 'If I whack out a million quid among those children, that might make a difference.' And then—*boom!*—like that, it was all gone. In that fucking crash. However, I've done it again. At my advanced age." My dad sat back in his chair and smiled with smug satisfaction.

I tried to process the information. Was my dad *really* saying that between the startup and the cancer, he didn't have time to care about his six kids?

I tried again. "The thing that upsets me is that you were never in contact with us," I said, "and you say that is because you had . . . other exciting stuff going on in your life?"

"Well, not necessarily exciting, but occupying all of one's attention," Dad said.

"But the shit that I went through from the time you went off to the time I left home!" I said. "Mom was so ill. And one day you were around, and you were this amazing, funny, wonderful dad, and the next you just weren't even there. . . ."

"Well, there we are," he said. "I regret that. I regret that. I regret that."

Another space opened up. *There. He said it. It's over. Walk away.*

There was another interminable pause, and then he said, "Sadly, we can't roll back the carpet."

Another even longer pause. Christ, this was like being in a Samuel Beckett play. Then he said, "Don't forget your fucking potato."

## 350 DAYS

I got back to New York and spent the next two freezing winter weeks in a daze, trying to make sense of my meeting with Dad, but there was nothing to make sense of. Nothing had changed. Nothing had been resolved. The words of the psychiatrist I had seen at Eton all those years ago kept ringing in my ears: "I can't just wave a magic wand and make all of this disappear." He was right. My dad was right. What's the point in being curious about something if you aren't going to have an answer?

I went to see Plum one afternoon while I was trying to work out how I felt. She had a new apartment in Greenwich Village. There was a fire crackling in the grate, and she made a cup of tea and asked how it went with Dad. What did I find out?

"Not much," I say. I stare intently into my teacup. I feel stupid. What a waste of time. What a waste of $700.

The log in the fire pops. And then Plum says something that completely blows my mind. She says, "I think it was a good thing that Dad left."

"What?" I say, baffled. *This is my great tragedy.*

"Yes," says Plum, sitting up now, cross-legged in her armchair, focused, holding her cup of tea. "You know how everyone said it was so unfortunate and so sad at the time?"

I nod dumbly.

"Well, privately, between themselves, some of them said to each other, 'Thank God that man has left Valerie and the children at last.'"

"What?" The world shifts under my feet. It feels like an ice floe breaking up or an earthquake cracking and resculpting the crust of the earth.

"Well, think about it, Tom," says Plum. "Do you really think it would have been a good thing for you to continue to be influenced by Dad? With his dishonesty, his affairs, his drinking? Would you be a writer? Would you be who you are? Would you be sober?"

"I don't know," I say. I stare at the shapes of the flames in the grate for ten seconds. Then I say, "Plum, I've got to go. I'm sorry. I'll call you later."

I actually feel sick as I get into the elevator. It takes an eternity for the doors to close. I walk down to the subway station and get the train home. I want to throw up because the world is spinning like it used to when I was drunk.

As I rattle up to Fifty-Fifth Street, I look back on my life, and that familiar, well-rehearsed story suddenly looks so different. It's like that moment when you are looking at a hologram, and you shift your head just a few degrees and a whole new picture emerges. And it's not done with a magic wand; it's just down to the way you are looking at it.

*I think it was a good thing Dad left.*

Plum might be right. Something I have always labeled "Bad Thing" might actually be a good thing. Or maybe it's not even a good thing. Maybe it's just something that happened, and that's just the way it is, and now it's time to get on with the rest of my life.

## 395 DAYS

I am not a regular visitor at the offices of the *New York Post* anymore. There's a new bar columnist, fresh-faced nightlife writers. I still contribute items to Page Six, but I've stopped working regular shifts there. I invent excuses to swing by and catch up with Chris and Paula whenever I can, though, because I miss them. I miss my old life. I miss getting drunk. I miss the exhilaration of losing control, the drama, the craziness, the screaming on the streets, the cabs, the cops, and the guns.

I went in one Wednesday, exactly fourteen months to the day since my last drink. My excuse was that I needed to pick up my mail. I didn't. I could tell by the branding on the outside of the envelopes what most of it was. A new vodka, a new bar, a launch party. I slid the whole lot into the trash unopened. *You're writing to the wrong man, guys.*

"So, what's going on?" said Chris.

"I'm heading back to Ireland tomorrow to catch up with Sasha," I said. "She went ahead yesterday."

"You're going away *again*?" asked Chris.

"Well, yeah. We're planning to spend a few months in Ireland once the baby comes. We want to try and rent a farmhouse for the summer where we could live."

Sasha was seven months pregnant now.

"You're going to go and live in *Ireland*?" Chris asked as his phone began to ring.

"Just for a few months," I replied defensively. "We're keeping the apartment here."

"So, you're leaving tomorrow," Chris stated. It wasn't a question. Both lines on his phone were ringing now.

Then I blurted out, "Hey, you want to go out tonight? Siberia?"

"Yeah, sure," said Chris, picking up his phone and putting his palm over the mouthpiece. "I have some big news to tell you."

"What?"

"It's big, man," laughed Chris. "Believe me, it's huge."

"I'll call you at around ten," I mouthed and headed off down the corridor in the direction of the elevator as he started talking on the phone.

Chris rang me at about quarter of ten. He was at a mutual friend's house in Greenwich Village having dinner. Did I want to come over? We could head out from there.

I jumped in a cab and tried not to think about how stupid I was being. My mouth watered every time I thought of a drink, the dry kick of a vodka, the satisfying bouquet of a glass of red wine.

*Stop it*, I thought to myself. *You're not going to drink and that's that.* But surely I *had* to be able to go into bars and clubs safely now. I had fourteen months sober. I'd been into a few bars in the past year, but never for much longer than I could avoid—half an hour or so max. Tonight was going to be a marathon in comparison.

The dinner party was in full swing when I arrived at the stylish and sumptuous two-story apartment on Sixth Avenue. There were eight people there, and dessert—olive oil ice cream delivered from Otto, a fancy Italian restaurant round the corner—was just being served. Most of the guests were still sitting around the large, wooden farmhouse table under a spiral staircase that led upstairs, but the focus of the party was shifting to the other end of the room, where a tall, pretty Russian dancer was chopping up some lines of cocaine on a glass-topped coffee table in front of an open fire.

"Vant a line?" she asked, all cheekbones and lips, as I walked in. It was the first thing anyone said to me. The coke looked kind of good, but Chris was already up out of his chair, coming toward me and replying for me. "No, man, he doesn't do that shit anymore." He stood up to give me a hug. "Good to see you, man."

Some of the guests started snorting lines. The host and hostess declined. Chris and I settled into the leather sofas around the fire. The host offered me a Diet Coke. He had a load in his fridge.

"So what's the big news?" I asked Chris as I poured Coke into a wine glass.

Chris smiled, took another sip of his glass of red wine, and smiled again. "You won't believe it, man. I'm dating a stripper."

"That's it?" I asked. "I was expecting you to tell me—I dunno—that you had a fancy new job or something."

"Man, you don't understand. This girl is a *Scores* stripper." He looked at me meaningfully. Scores was a chain of flashy lap-dancing clubs in the city. "That means she is one of the hottest strippers in the world. And she is dating *me*."

Chris shook his head smugly. "I mean, it's *ridonculous,* dude. We are different life forms. I'm a monkey and she is a goddess. She tans. She drinks juice. She has this perfect, flat belly. It's a model banging a monkey."

We hung around at the party till about midnight, by which time the host was ushering his guests out of the door. He wiped the coke crumbs off the table with an old cloth and a look of disdain. He saw me catch his expression and said, "I mean, it's *Wednesday.*"

He sat down next to me and sighed. "Don't you find drunk people really boring now?" he asked.

"Well, I don't hang around with them when they are actually

*drunk* very much anymore," I said. "But yeah, it's kind of tedious sometimes. People high on coke are the worst. When someone you hardly know gets on a coke-a-log and invites you on holiday, that's when it's time to leave."

He laughed. "Do you get tempted to drink?"

"Sometimes. But I don't really get tempted to drink at parties or bars anymore just because I think it would be fun. Now, I want to drink when I get scared."

I was thinking of the night before my grandmother's funeral a few months earlier, when I was staying in my brother Fred's room, and I got a major craving in the night. I was feeling desperately guilty about how I had wasted all the money from the house she had given me. I had betrayed my wonderful grandmother, who had done so much for me and my family, and now she was dead. I had to go and wake up my other brother, Josh, at three in the morning and get him to hide a bottle of whiskey that was sitting on the shelf of Fred's room.

"Maybe it's time for us to go as well," I said. "Chris, you ready?"

"Yeah, man, let's go," he yelled, draining his wine glass. "Siberia, one last time. Who's coming?"

It was just the two of us.

Still, it was fun, riding uptown with Chris wisecracking all the way, boasting about his new girlfriend, and then rocketing out of the cab when we got to our destination so he didn't have to pay the fare. Just like old times, I thought, as I paid up and asked for a receipt.

Siberia was exactly the way it was when I left. The floor was the texture of molasses. Nirvana was blasting out of the jukebox. Patrick was still behind the bar. One difference was a brand-new pinball machine winking away where the Pac-Man I had demolished fourteen months earlier once stood.

"So, you got a new pinball machine," I said to Gareth, an Irish guy who sometimes worked for Tracey at Siberia as an electrician. He was a regular, but he didn't remember me.

"Oh, yeah," Gareth said. "It's only about two weeks old, that one. The old one got smashed."

I frowned. Hang on, this was a new *new* pinball machine?

"How did the other one get smashed?" I asked.

"Well, it involved a lot of drink," Gareth said, speaking frenetically. "A big hairy man threw a cash register at the wall, that wall over there, and it was going so fast that it ricocheted off and hit the glass. But it was like safety glass, so it didn't smash properly, so he went over and smashed it up with his head." Gareth smiled.

"A big, hairy man?" I asked in disbelief. "Tracey? Tracey smashed up his *own* pinball machine in his *own* bar? That's pure Siberia."

"You see, man?" exclaimed Chris, swigging on a beer. "You see how little it matters what you did smashing up that Pac-Man? Personally, I was like, 'Big deal,' but *you* took it as a sign from God. You were totally premature."

We were standing by the bar when Tracey walked in, at about half past midnight. I gave a roar of greeting. Tracey came over, bearhugged me, then pointed to the person with him and said, "Hey, man, this is my son."

I shook hands with his son, then we walked to the back of the bar and sat on two leather sofas set at right angles to each other. There were no more than six other people in the bar—Chris, Gareth, and another former barman, Kieran, who had come in with a few girls who were hanging around by the Harleys.

"So I heard you got sober," Tracey came out with it right away. "You're a better man than most, and I hope when it's my turn, I am man enough to quit."

"Thanks, Tracey," I muttered. I always get embarrassed when people congratulate me on my sobriety. First, I feel that I didn't really have much to do with it, that it just kind of happened; and second, I worry about that being one more person to laugh at me if I ever drink again.

"Was I really bad? Even by Siberia standards?" I asked him.

"Look, man," said Tracey, "I run another bar round the corner called Bellevue. That's named after the city psych ward. We have people who show up there asking for Dr. Katz. We don't deal with dead-on knuckleheads, but you were pretty far out there."

"And the night I smashed up the Pac-Man? What did you think then?"

Tracey pulled on his goatee and considered his answer carefully. "That thing was there for nine years. And you were the only person to break it. So you've got to figure, first," he pushed his right thumb into his left palm, "first, it's not very easy to break, and second," he marked the point with his index finger, "second, how far out have you got to be to do something like that? So it's good you chilled the fuck out, because you could have done something to hurt someone or yourself. Most likely yourself."

As Tracey was talking, we were suddenly enveloped by a strong petrochemical smell.

Tracey leapt up out of the sofa with amazing alacrity given his massive bulk and yelled, "Who's spraying shit in here?"

Gareth was standing by the Harleys looking guilty. "Someone knocked over the Harley," he said. "And gas came out."

"It's not supposed to having fucking gas in it!" yelled Tracey. Then he turned to me. "I've got my son with me. We've got to get out of here. I'm not about to get crisped in a bar with my son."

We went outside with Chris and Gareth. I had a cigarette while Tracey carried on talking about my drinking. "The thing is, Tom, I'd see you hit that switch, and you'd just go into another world. You went over the edge," he said.

I told him about that night in Siberia, when I had thought I was Ozzy Osbourne and had my out-of-body experience.

"I'm really sorry about the Pac-Man," I said. "Do I owe you for it?"

"What you can do for me is give your wife a kiss and stay away from the whiskey. That's your payback to me. Come on. Let's go to Bellevue and let the fumes clear out."

An hour or so later, Chris and I were sitting at the bar in the joint next door to Bellevue. I asked him, "So, when are you going to give up drinking, man?"

"When I die," said Chris and slugged back his vodka and tonic. "I can't imagine a life without alcohol. I can't give it up ever."

It was 1:30 a.m. "I miss you," he said. "You were one of my best friends, and we were just raging . . . animals. I thought I loved this guy and he's gone. I miss you, man."

"I miss you too, Chris," I said, shaking my head. "I miss it all. You know what I miss most? I miss the never quite knowing what is going to happen or where you're going to end up."

We sat in silence for a few moments.

"Let's get out of here," I said.

We headed for the door and stood on the pavement for a few moments.

"Wanna go to Bungalow?" said Chris after a few seconds.

"Bungalow? I dunno. You're kind of wasted. . . ."

Chris came up close to me, his face within inches of my own. "This is what we used to be like all the time, bro," he said.

"There is that, I guess," I said. Chris and I were not going to be refused entry anywhere. "Let's go."

We got into a cab, but as we were speeding down Ninth Avenue, Chris said, "If we go to Marquee, we'll get our own table and bottles. Shall we do Marquee instead?"

"Okay," I said. "You think they'll let you in?"

"Of course, man! I'll just walk to the front of the line and go, 'Yo! Richie! What's up?' And *bam!* We'll go straight in."

We pulled up outside Marquee, and Chris pulled open the street-side door and climbed out. The taxi driver started to yell at him to get out the other side, but Chris just muttered, "I'll cut your throat."

I paid the cab, and Chris and I walked to the front of the line. As Chris had predicted, we said, "Yo! Richie! What's up?" and went right in.

Noah Tepperberg, the owner of the club, was waiting for us when we walked in. He was always there when you walked in, because he spent the night watching the door line on CCTV in a side office, radioing instructions to the doorman on which wannabes to let in and to bounce.

He hugged me hello, then shouted over the booming sound system, "You guys want a table?"

"Sure," shouted Chris, and we followed Noah to one of the prized tables in the center of the club. The space was packed with stunning twenty-four-year-old girls dressed in almost nothing and older, richer guys dressed in suits and hipsters in T-shirts and jeans. A lithe waitress brought over a bottle of vodka and an ice bucket filled with champagne and beer and set them on the low table in front of us. I ordered a glass of Coke.

"You want anything else, let me know," she said, flashed us a mile-wide smile, and disappeared into the writhing crowd. There would be no check tonight. Not for Page Six.

The bottle whores began swarming our table in search of a free drink. We handed out beers and champagne and vodka cranberries. Chris had been playfighting all night, but now the punches were starting to get just a little harder. I noticed a smartly dressed blond guy in a suit and tie standing by our table. He had been following me and Chris wherever we went. Who was this dude?

I sat down on the back of the banquette at our table with my feet on the seat. Noah came up and sat next to me. We chatted for a bit, then I said, "Who's that blond guy who keeps following us around?"

Noah laughed and said, "That's your security detail."

"What?" I said.

"I always get a security guard to tail you guys around to make sure you don't hurt yourselves," said Noah as Chris started laying into Paolo Zampolli, the head of I.D. models, pushing and play-punching him way too hard.

"And you do all that, put up with all that shit, gave me all that license just because I worked on Page Six?" Paolo Zampolli was fighting his way across the dance floor away from Chris. In fact, a space had opened up in a four-foot radius around Chris, the only space in the entire club. It reminded me of when you think you've miraculously found a seat on a crowded subway, but when you get there, there's vomit on the floor.

Noah flinched. "Not just because of Page Six but because you were one of my buddies," he said, looking hurt. "All the press get some license, but you guys are friends. So you always got special treatment."

Chris was standing at the table pouring himself another vodka with painstaking attention, glass and bottle both at eye level. Noah started ordering some more drinks from the hostess for the table.

"Do you want something, Tom?"

"Just another Diet Coke, please, Noah," I said. Then I looked at my watch. It was three. I didn't need another Diet Coke. It was way, way past time for me to go as it was. "Actually, forget it, I'm fine," I said.

I went over to Chris, gave him a hug, and said, "Look after your-self, mate. I've got to go."

"I love you, man," he slurred. We hugged. "This is it, man. I'm never going to see you again," said Chris.

"Of course we'll see each other again," I said. But I knew what he meant. The Tom Sykes he was talking about was last seen demolish-ing a Pac-Man fourteen months ago in Siberia.

I got my coat and left Marquee for the last time.

It was cold outside, and it felt good to be in the fresh air. My head felt thick and heavy from the music, the smoke, and the dancing. I could guarantee I would have a phantom hangover tomorrow.

There was still a mob of two hundred people or so desperate to get into Marquee and take my place. They were coming up with all the lines.

"My boyfriend's inside. . . ."

"Noah's expecting me. . . ."

"We've got a table reservation. . . ."

"I just came out for a cigarette. . . ."

Nightlife is big business. Casualties like me, well, we're just natural wastage.

## 396 DAYS

I'm in a cab on the way to the airport the next afternoon, looking forward to seeing Sasha, wondering what sex our baby will be, and realizing I don't care just, please God, let it be healthy. My phone rings. It's Chris.

I pick up. "Wilson?"

"Mr. Sykes," he says, his voice crackly and dry and hungover.

"How are you?" I ask.

"Oh, my God," he croaks. "I feel like a bear shat in my head. But I have just one question for you. What did I do last night?"